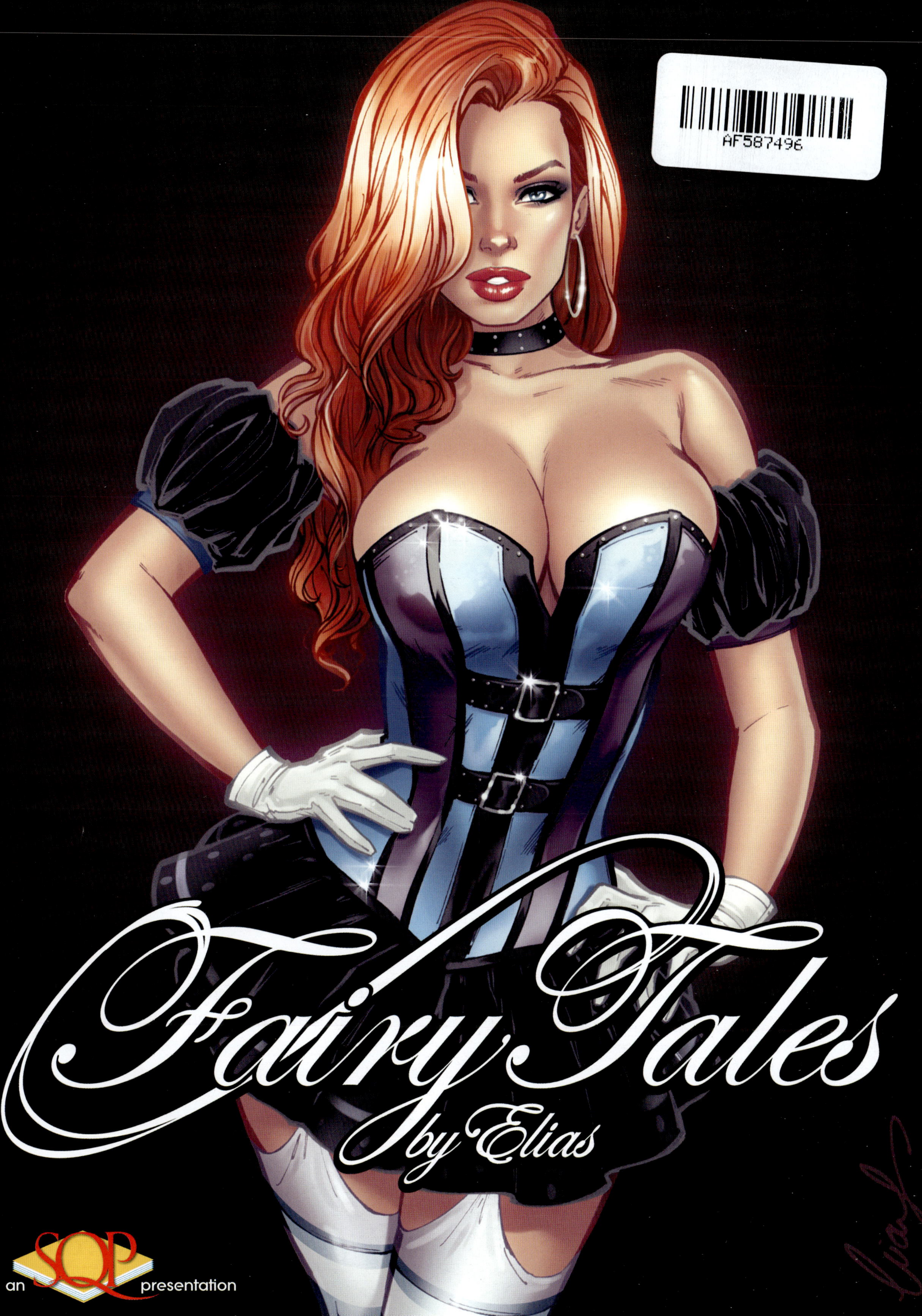

Fairy Tales
by Elias
an SQP presentation

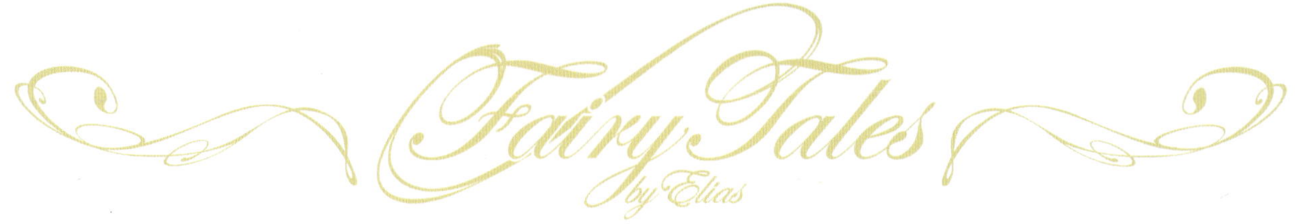

English

Hi,

My name is Elias Chatzoudis and I've officially been creating pinup girls since 2005. I work with advertising companies and artists and with comic-book publishers, mainly on covers. Fairy Tales by Elias is an idea I had some time ago and I'm very lucky to be producing it in partnership with S.Q. Productions, so that after "Fever Pitch 1" and "Fever Pitch 2" we have created an album of your favourite heroines from well-known fairy-tales, giving them with a more adult, sexy look. In Fairy Tales by Elias you can see the original ink or pencil drawings and the final computer-coloured versions.

French

Salut,

Je m'appelle est Elias Chatzoudis et je m'occupe des pin-up girls, officiellement, depuis 2005, je collabore avec des agences de publicité et des artistes ainsi qu'avec des entreprises qui publient des bandes dessinées, principalement, des couvertures d'ouvrages. 'Fairy Tales by Elias' est une idée que j'avais depuis quelque temps et je suis particulièrement heureux de la réaliser en collaboration avec S.Q. Productions. Ainsi, après les "Fever Pitch 1" et "Fever Pitch 2", nous avons créé un album avec mes héroïnes préférées de contes de fées populaires, vues sous un angle plus adulte et sexy. Dans 'Fairy Tales by Elias', vous verrez les dessins originaux, réalisés à l'encre ou au crayon, ainsi que leur forme finale, en couleur, sur ordinateur.

Spanish

Hola,

Me llamo Elias Chatzoudis y llevo creando pinup girls desde 2005; colaboro con empresas de publicidad y con artistas, así como con editoriales de cómics, para las que elaboro portadas, principalmente. Fairy Tales by Elias es una idea que tenía desde hace tiempo y me alegra mucho llevarla a cabo con la colaboración de S.Q. Productions. Después de Fever Pitch 1 y Fever Pitch 2 hemos creado un álbum con mis protagonistas preferidas de los cuentos clásicos vistas desde un ángulo adulto y sexy. En Fairy Tales by Elias se pueden ver los bocetos originales a tinta o lápiz además de su versión definitiva coloreada por ordenador.

Happily Ever After...

Fairy Tales by Elias

Book design by Elias Chatzoudis.

Published by SQP Inc.
PO Box 248 - Columbus NJ 08022

Sal Quartuccio & Bob Keenan - Publishers

For a free, full color catalog showcasing the entire SQP line of erotic, fantasy, and pin-up artwork, go to:
www.sqpartbooks.com

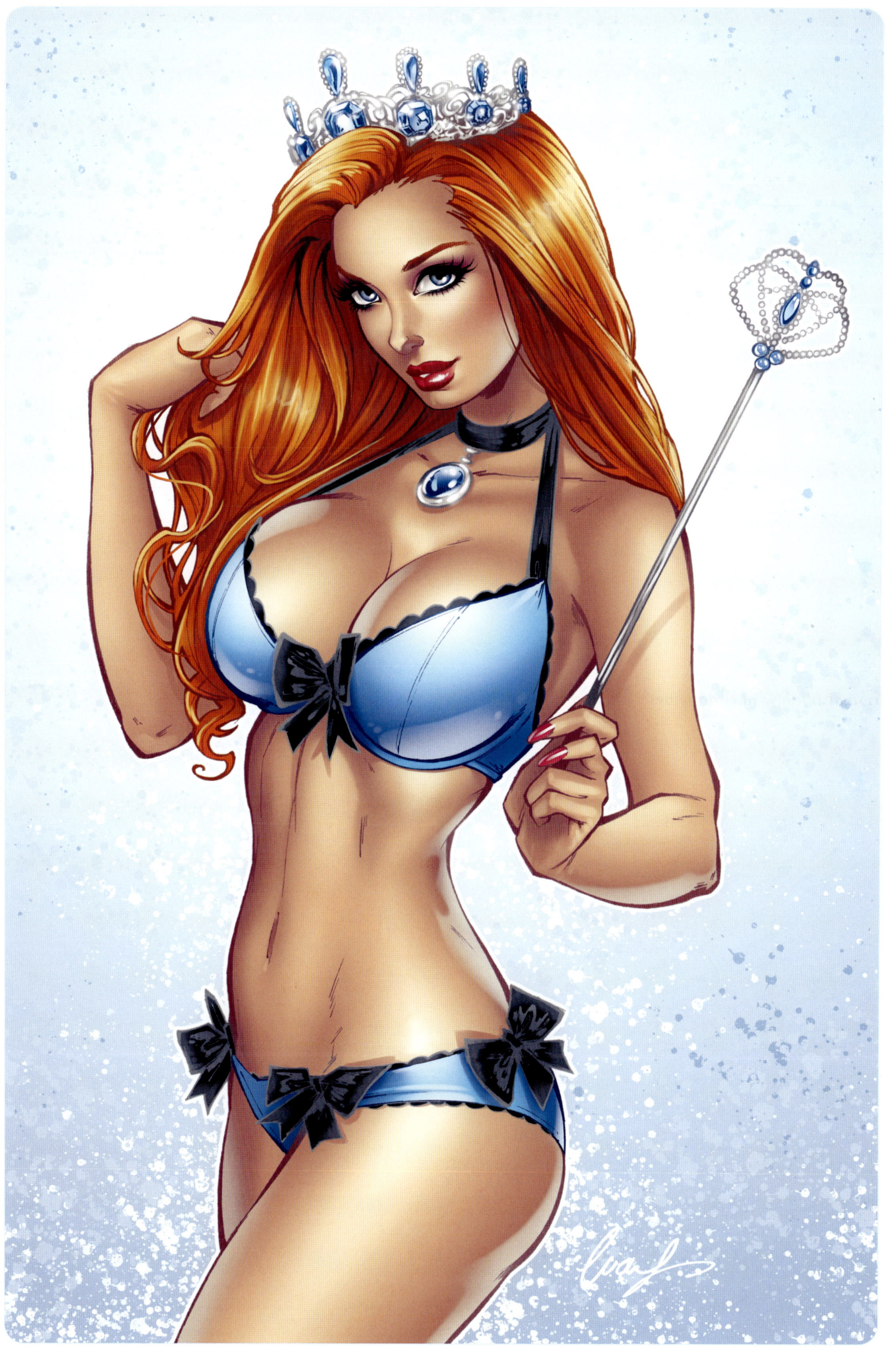

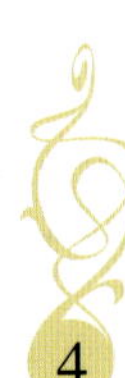

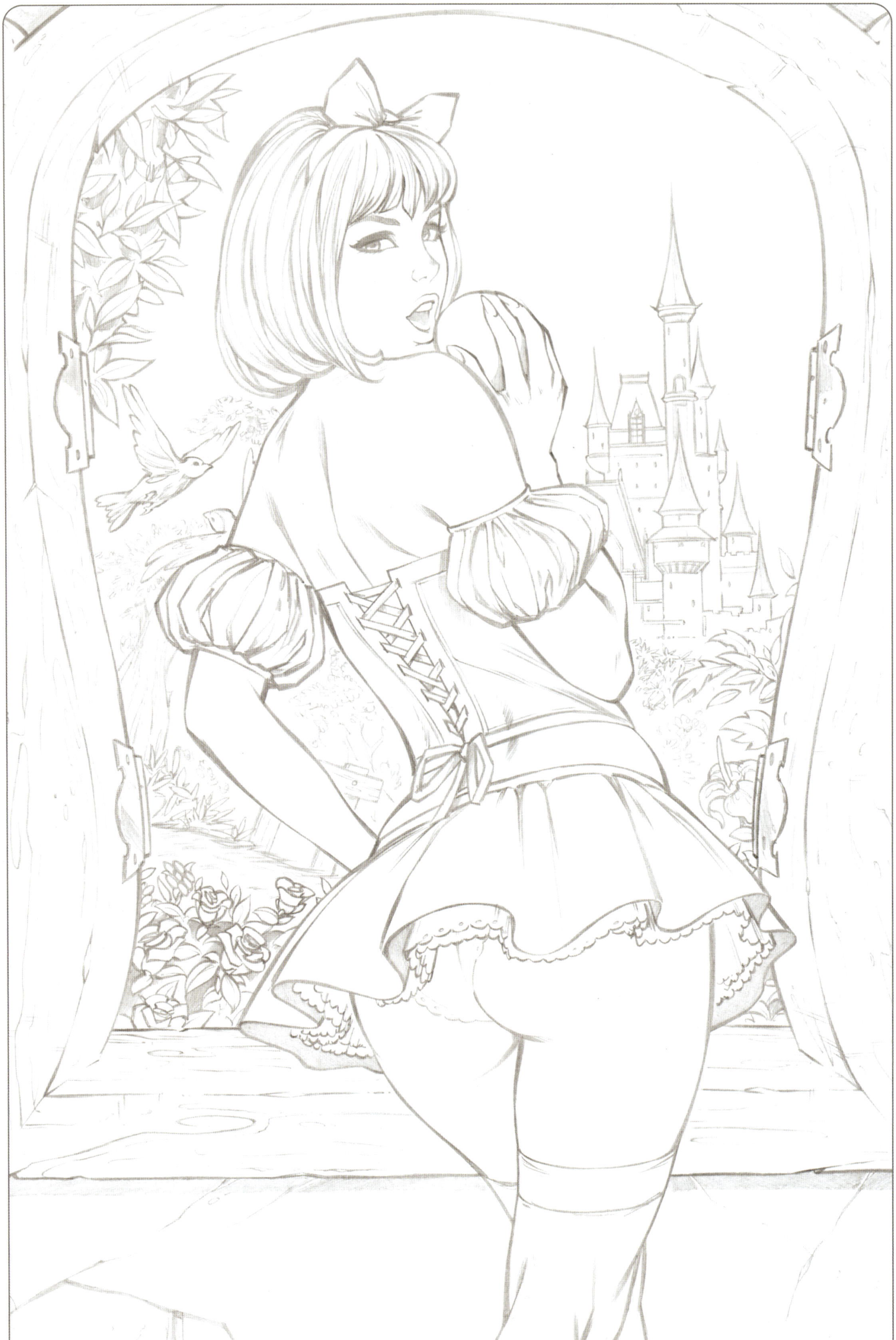

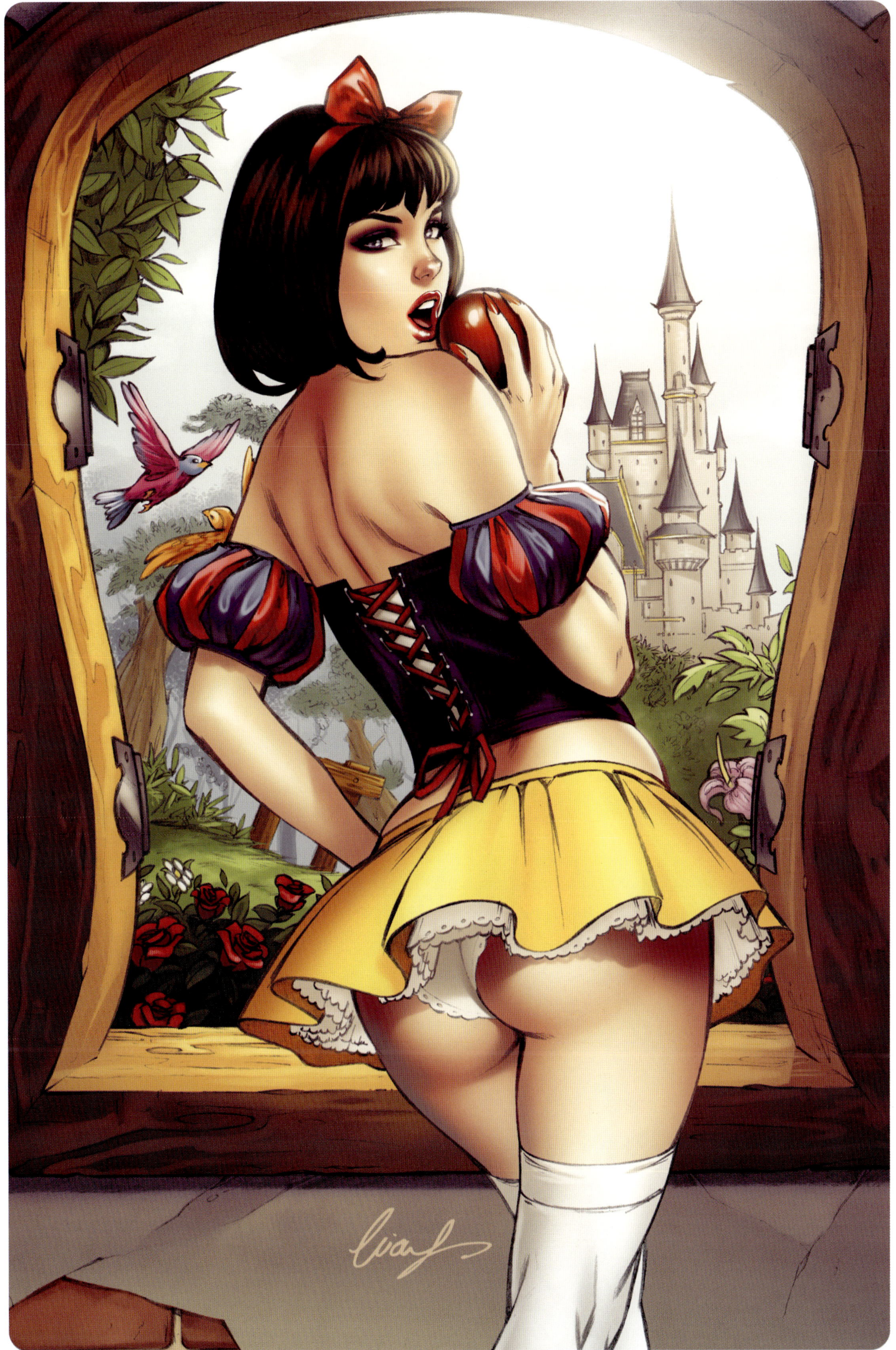

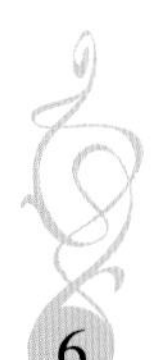

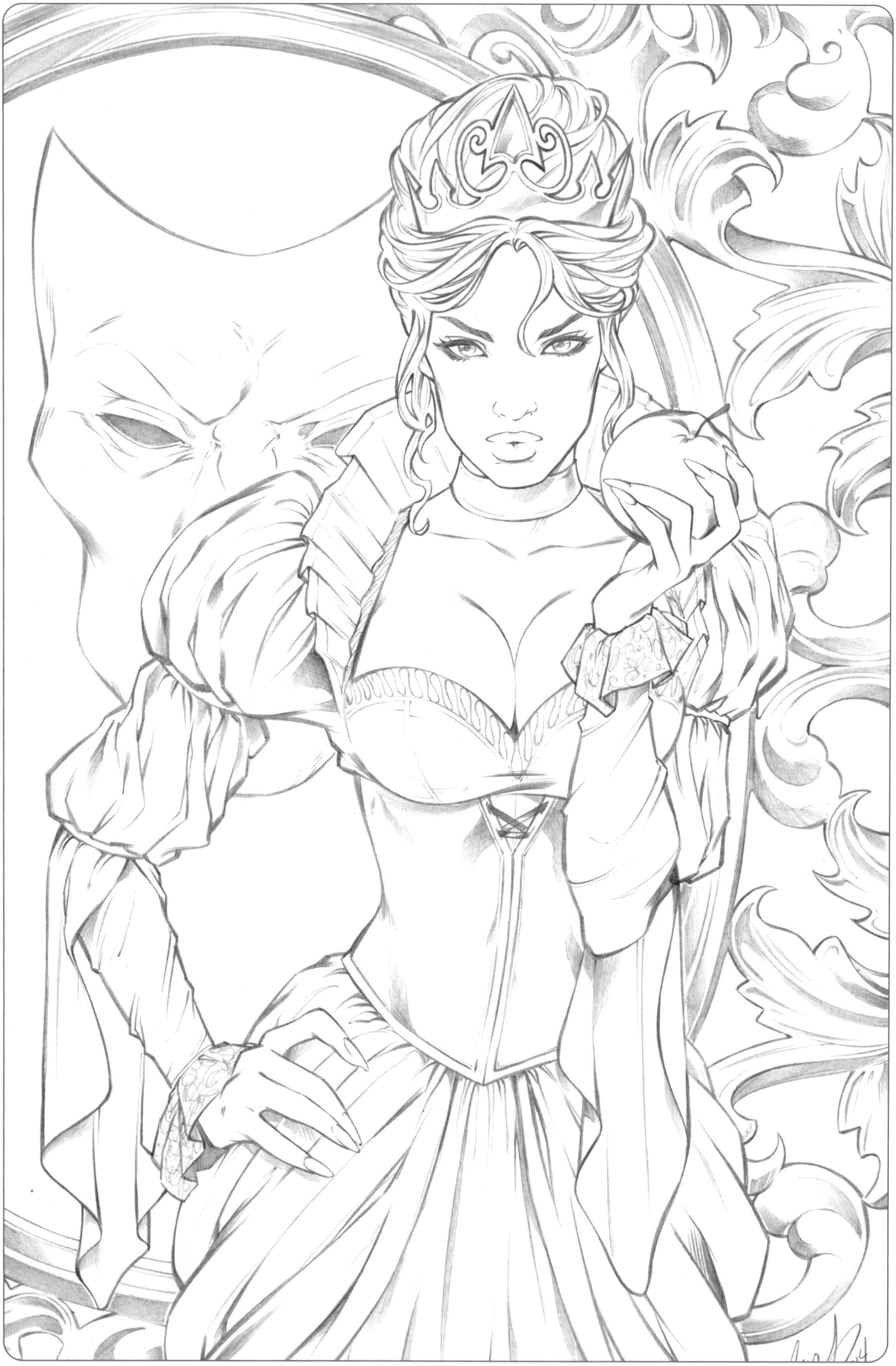

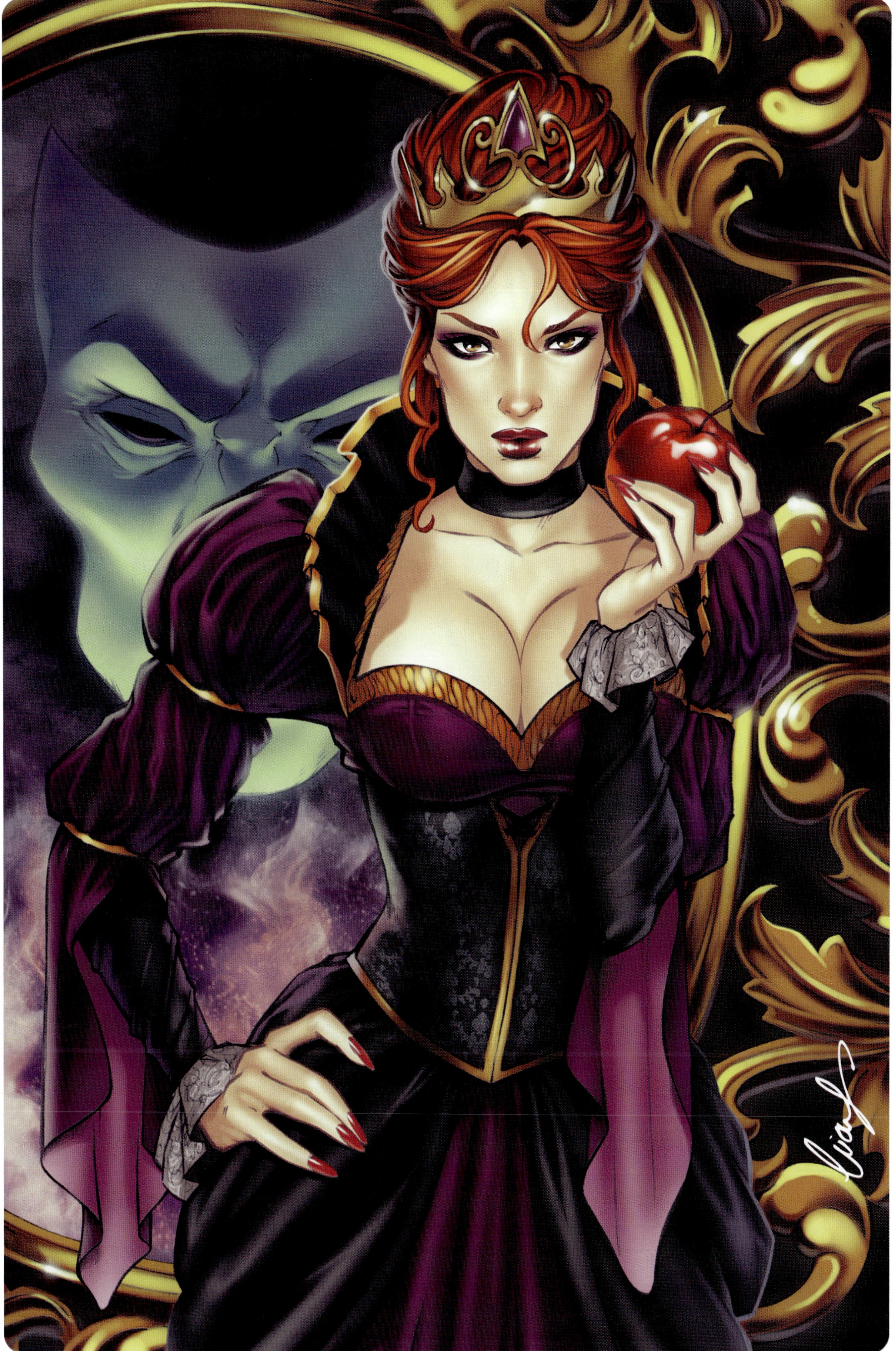

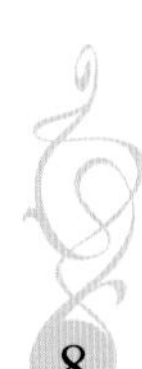

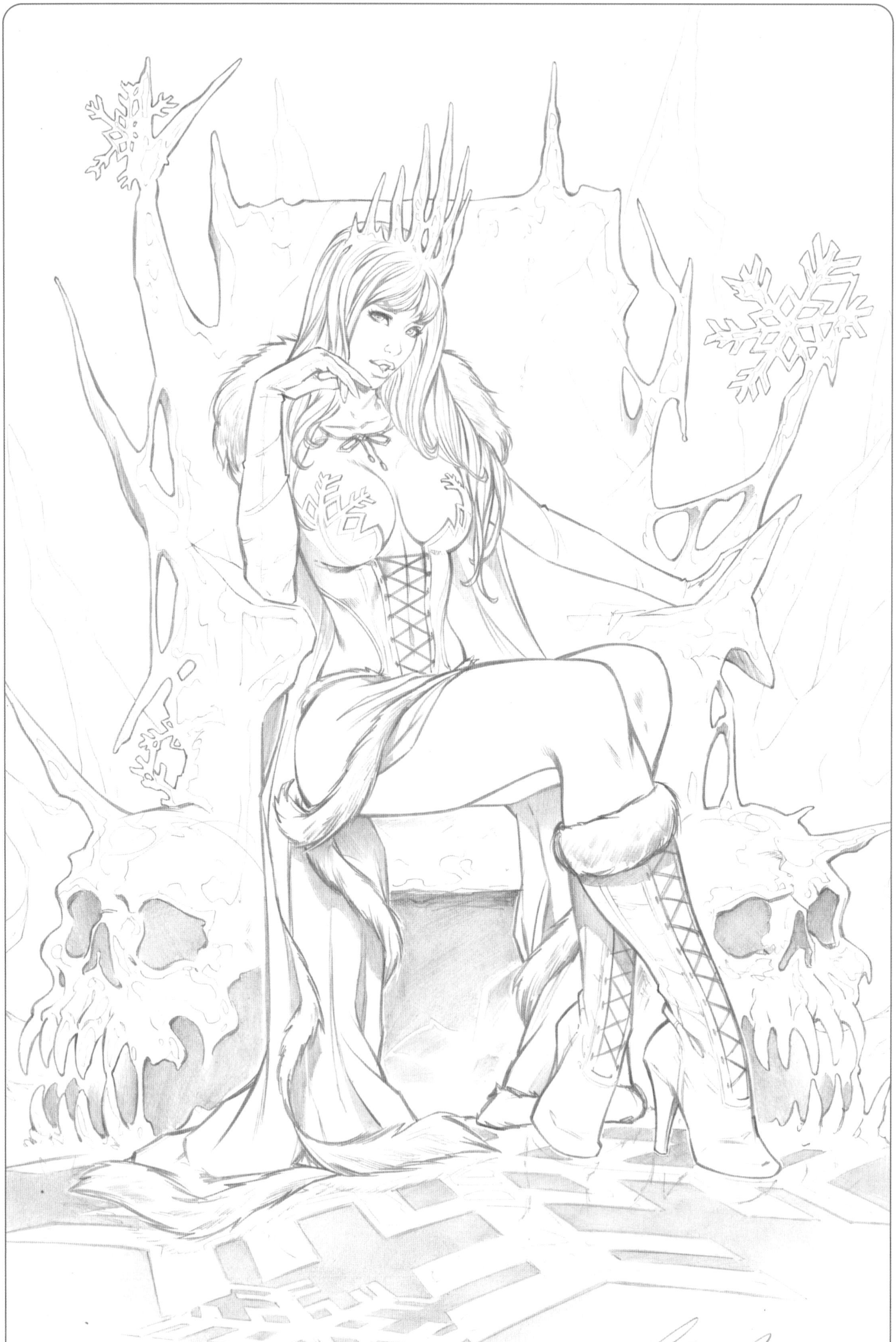

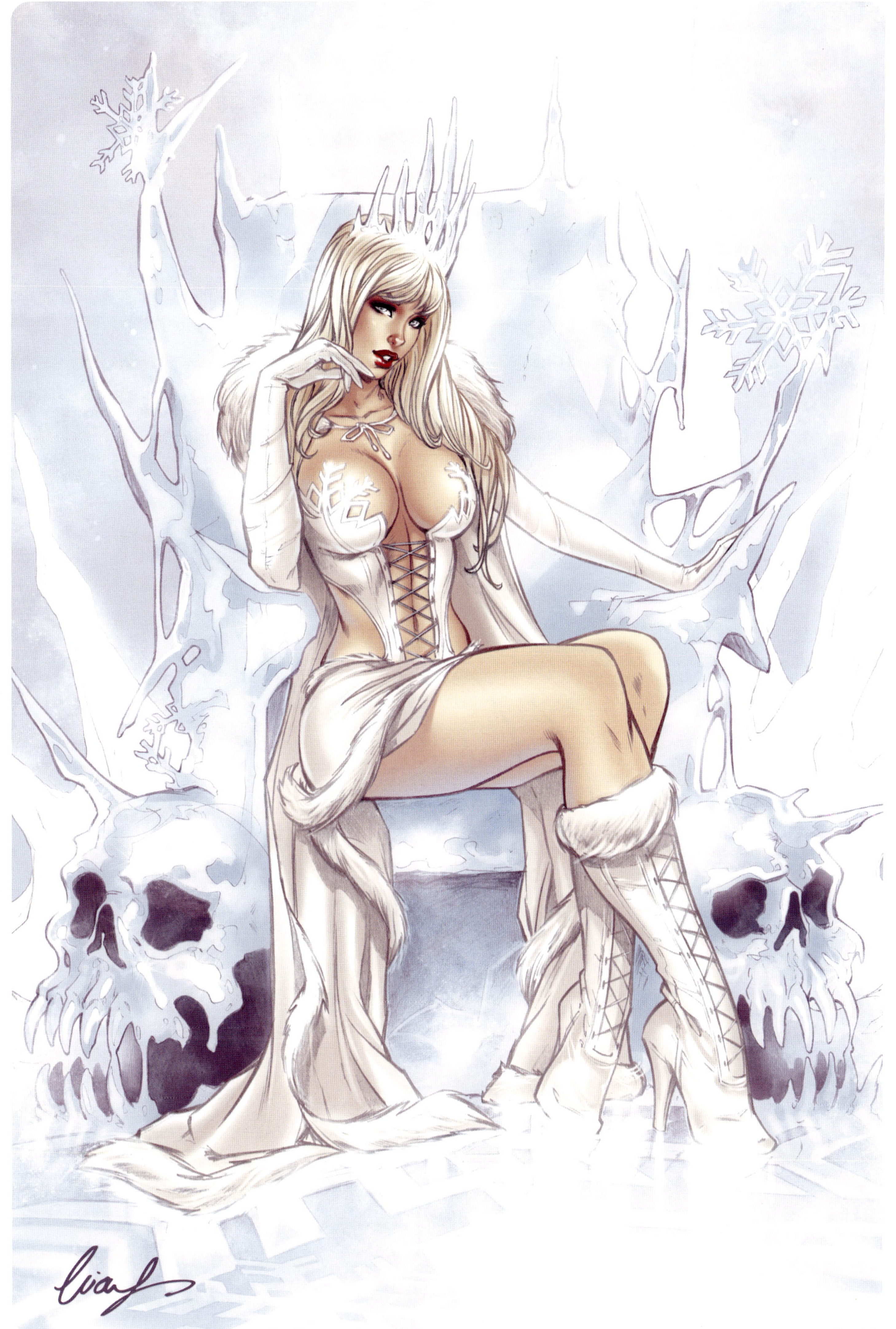

Snow Queen

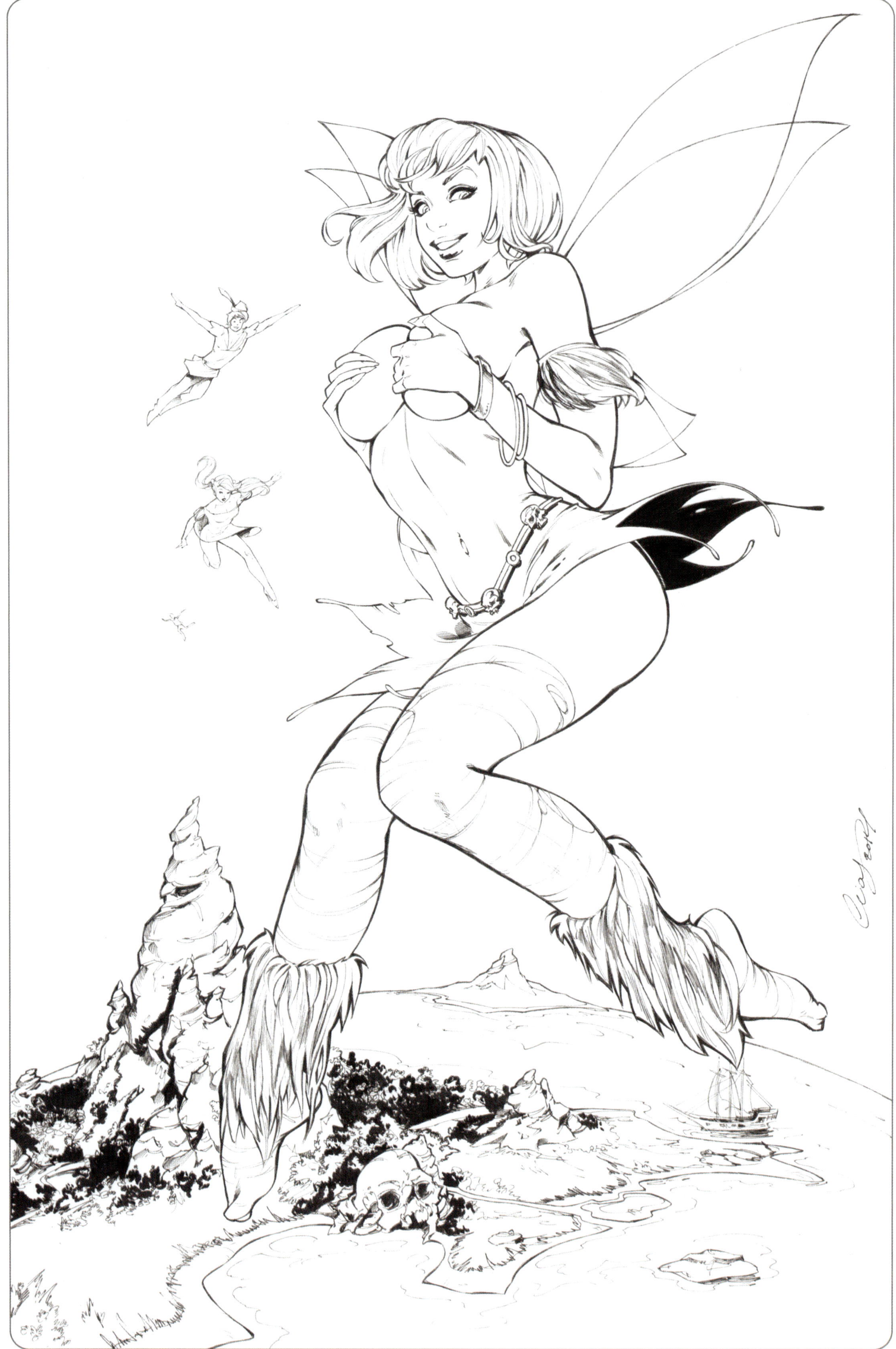

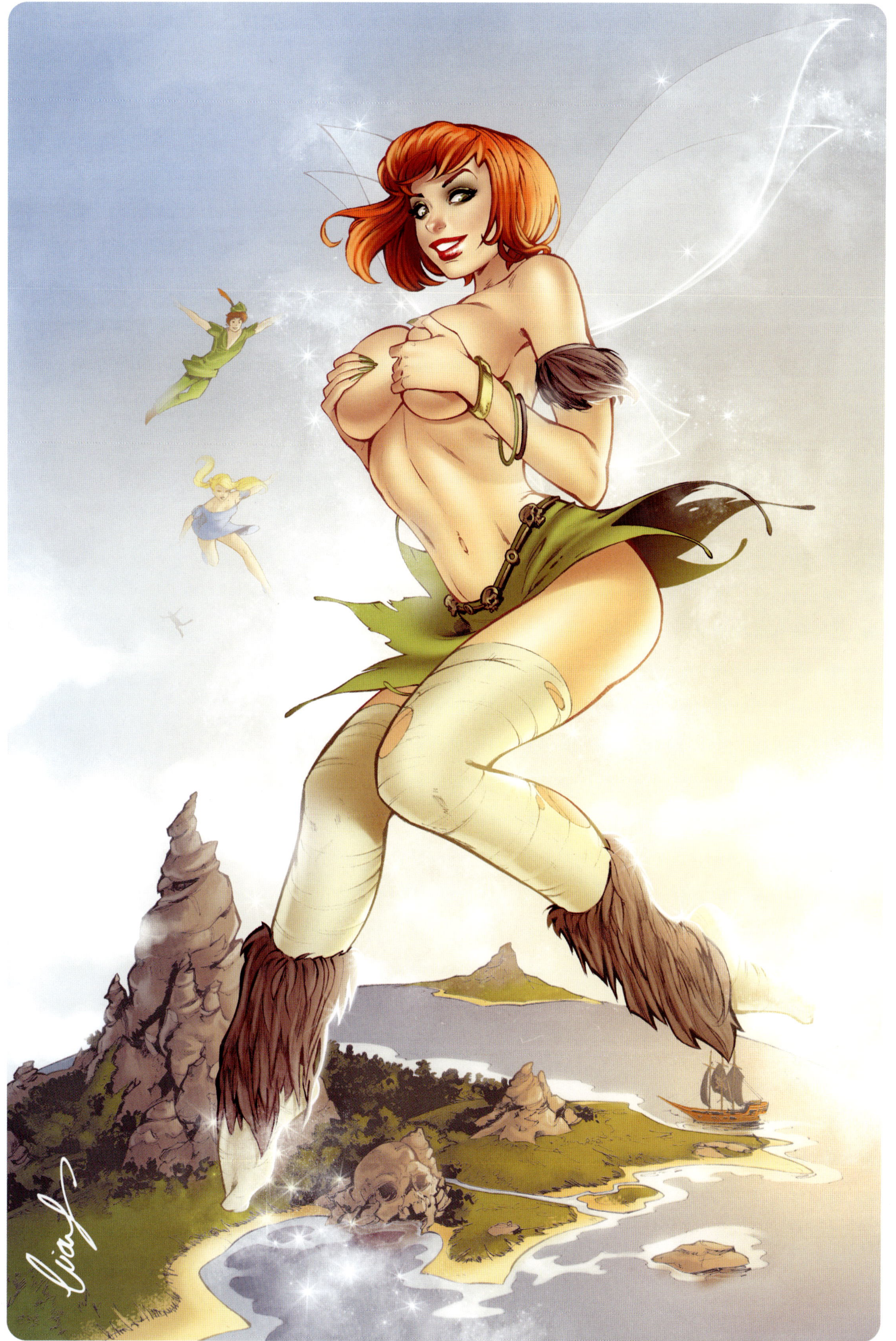

Tinkerbell

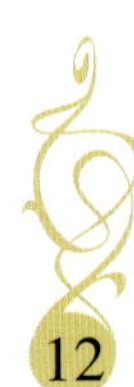

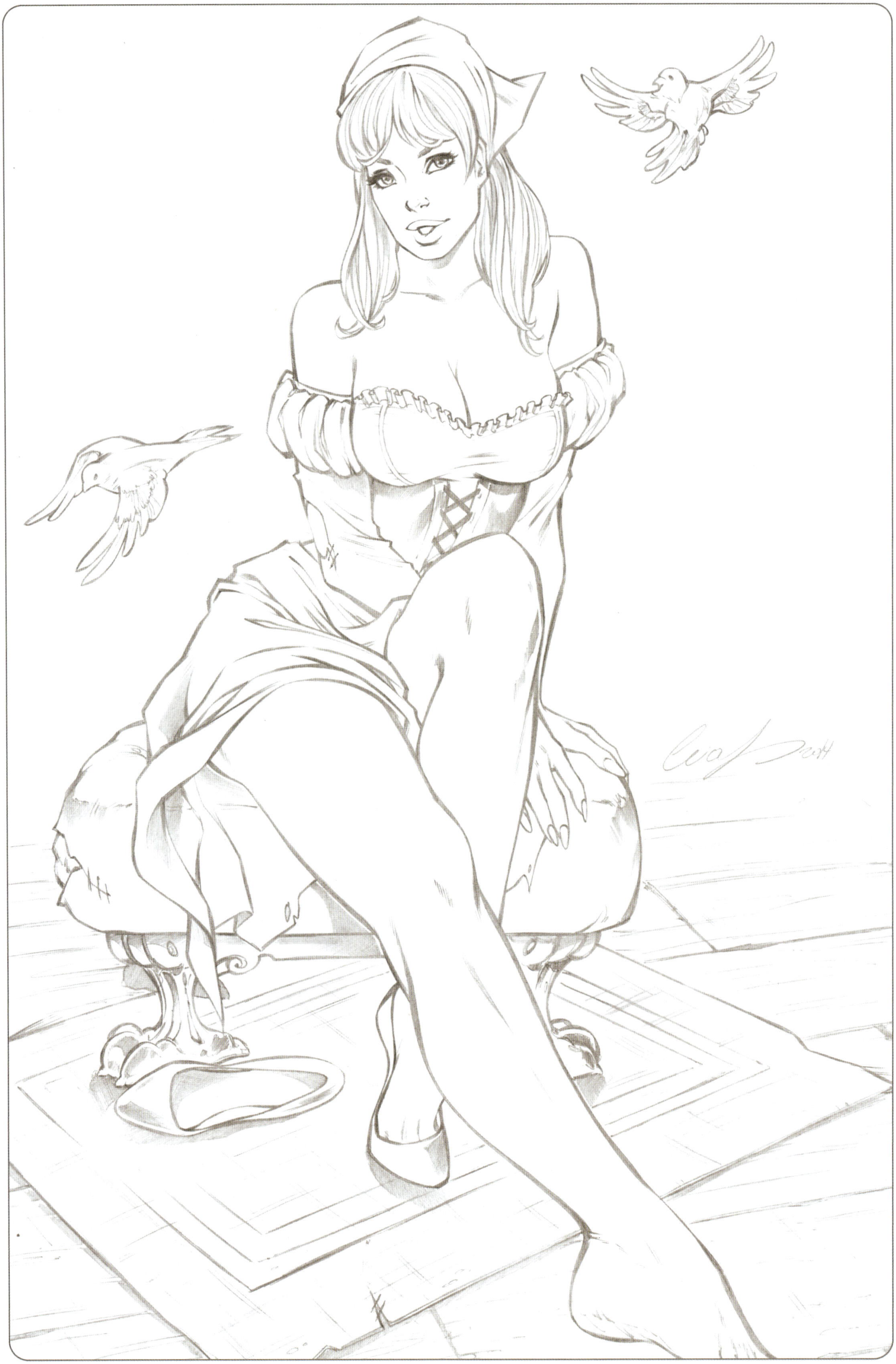

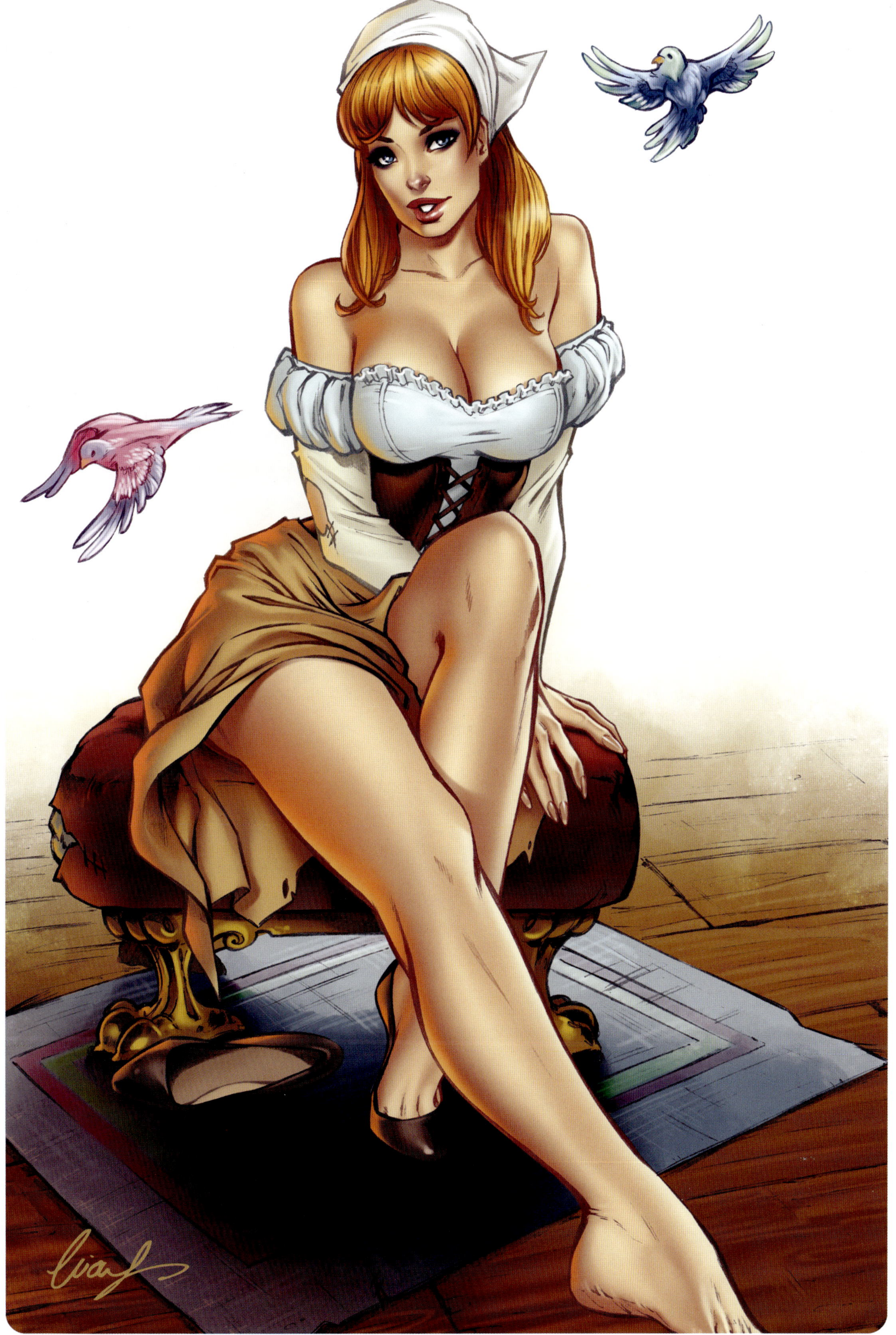

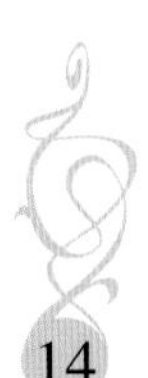

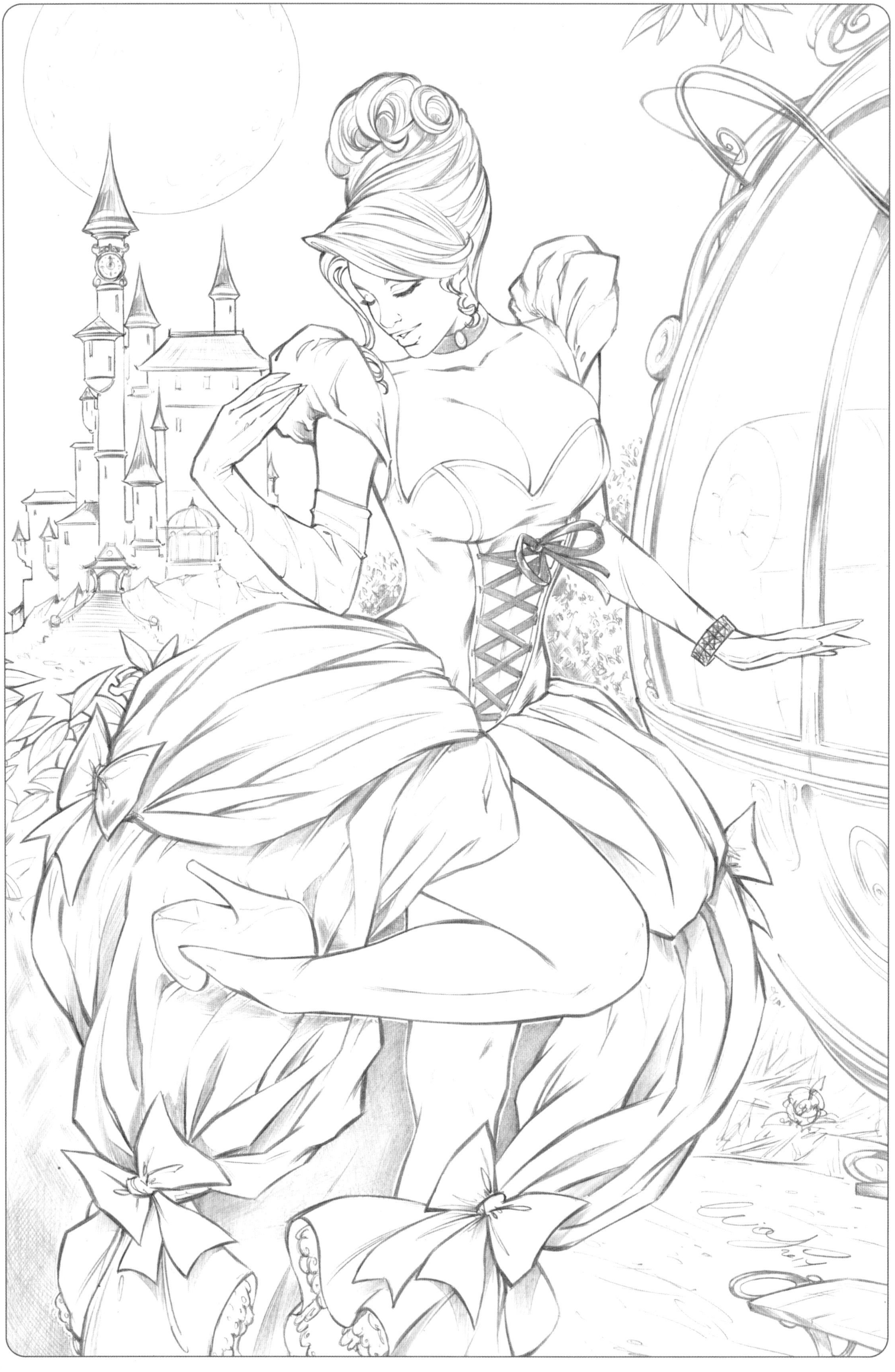

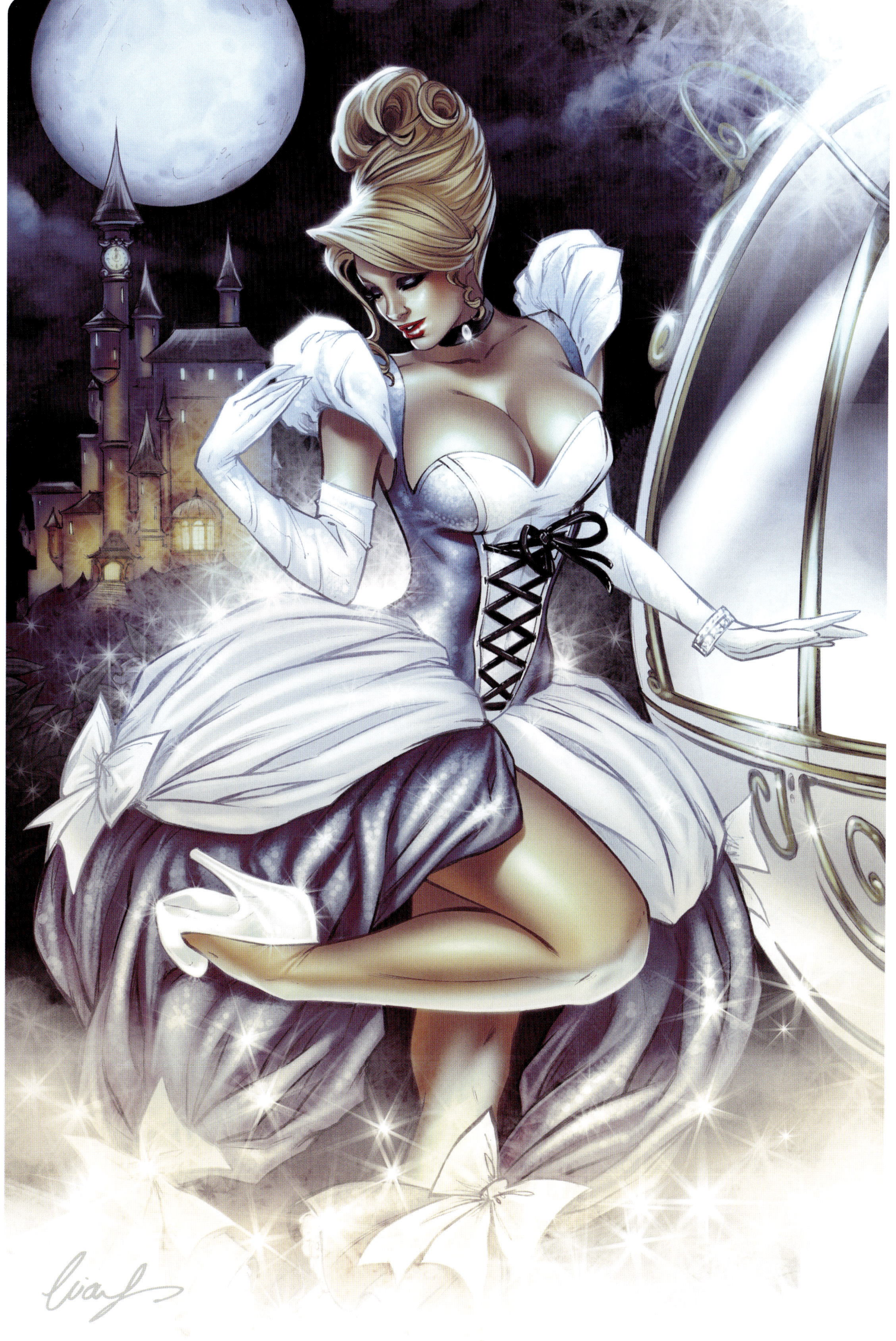

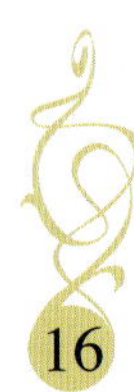

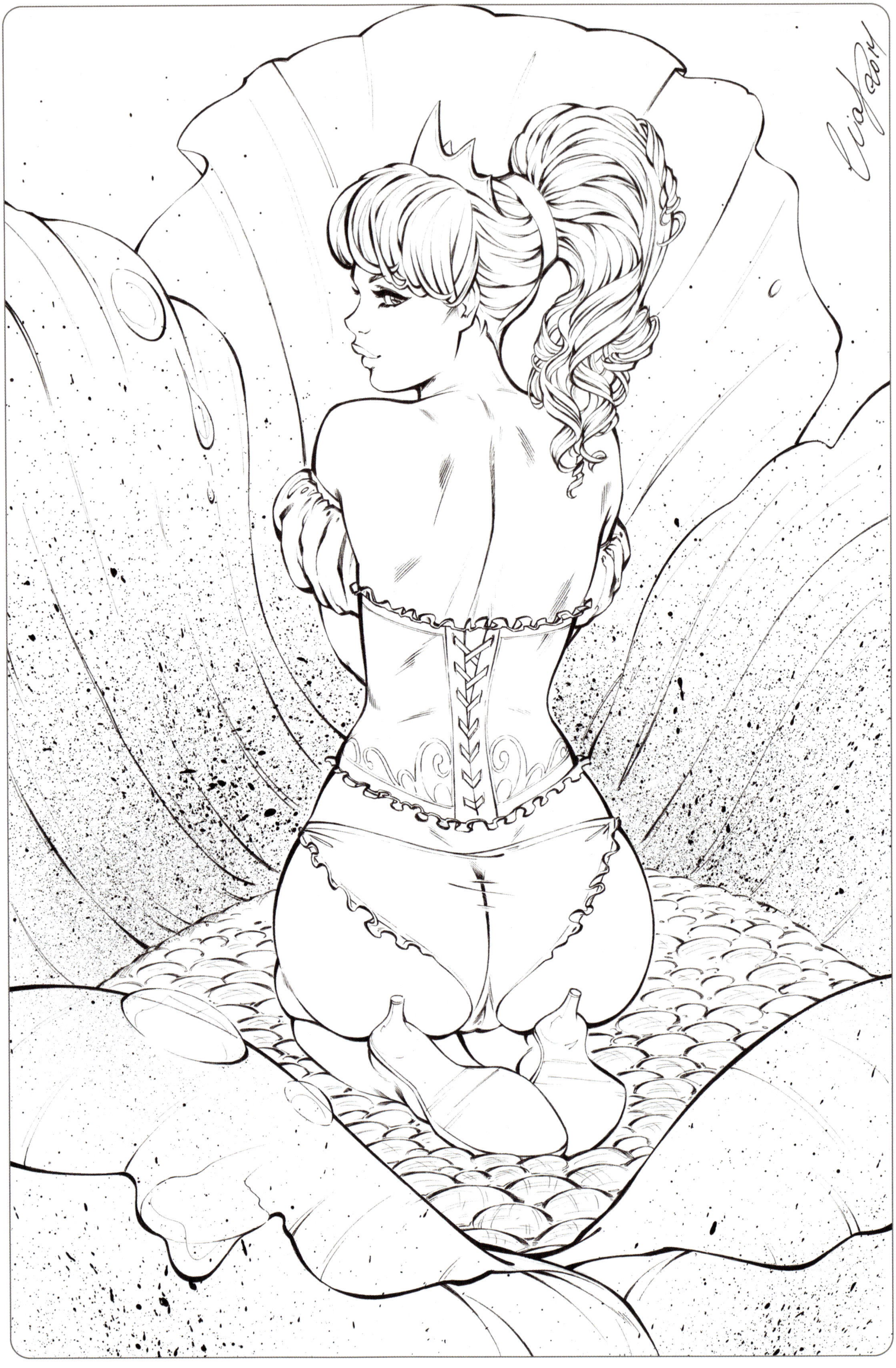

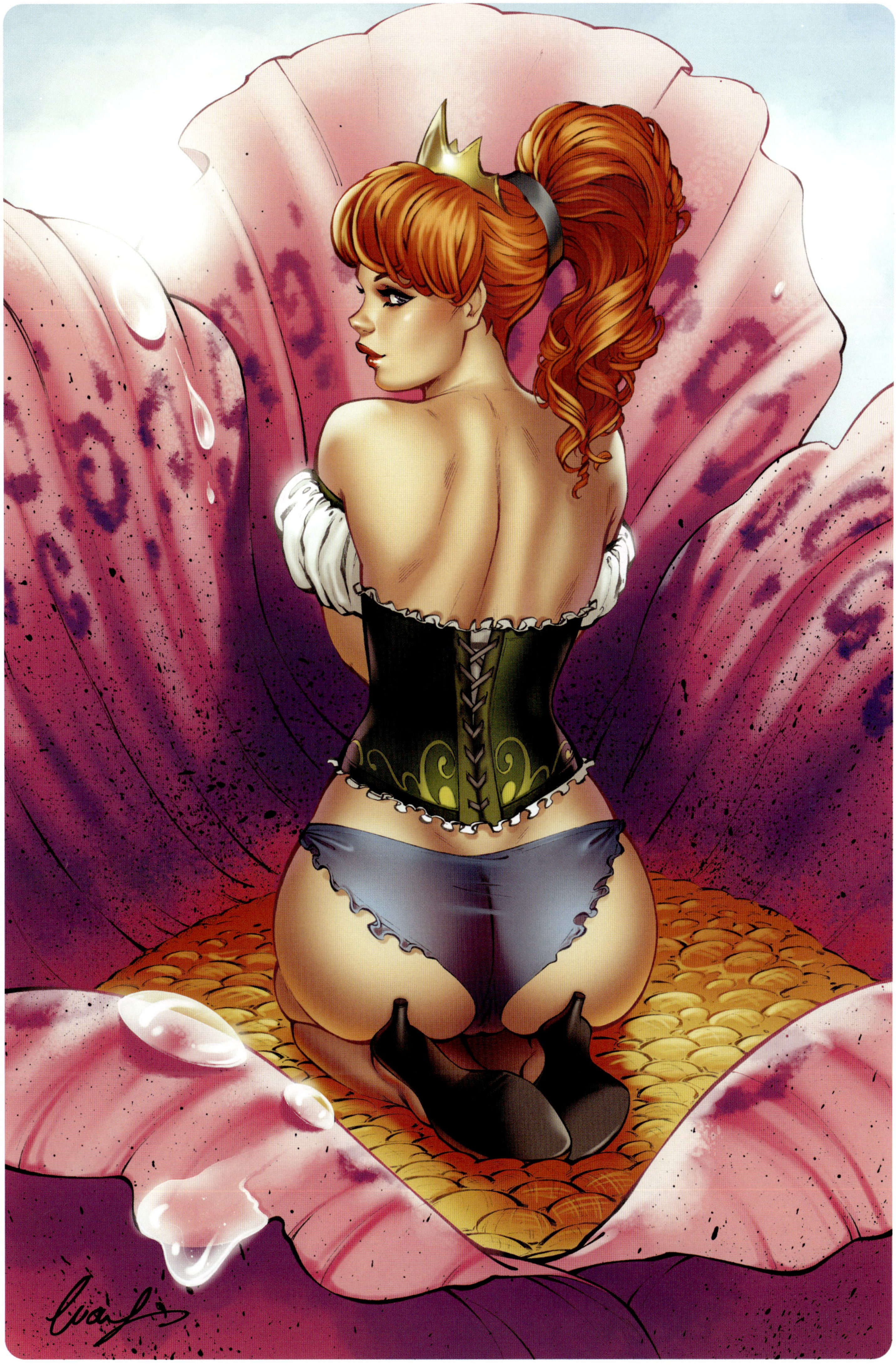

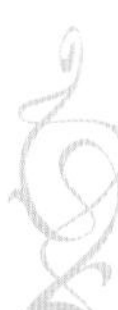

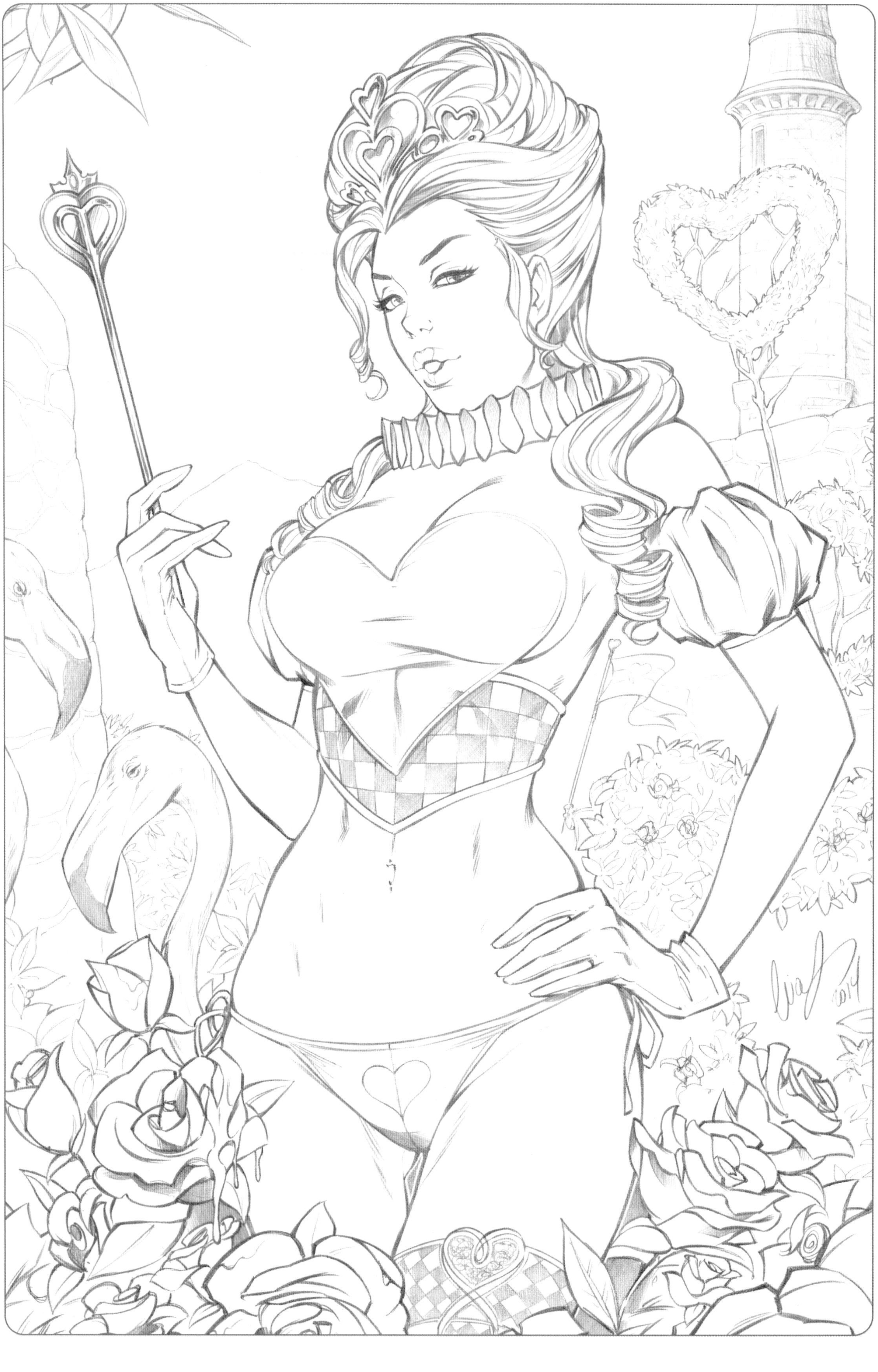

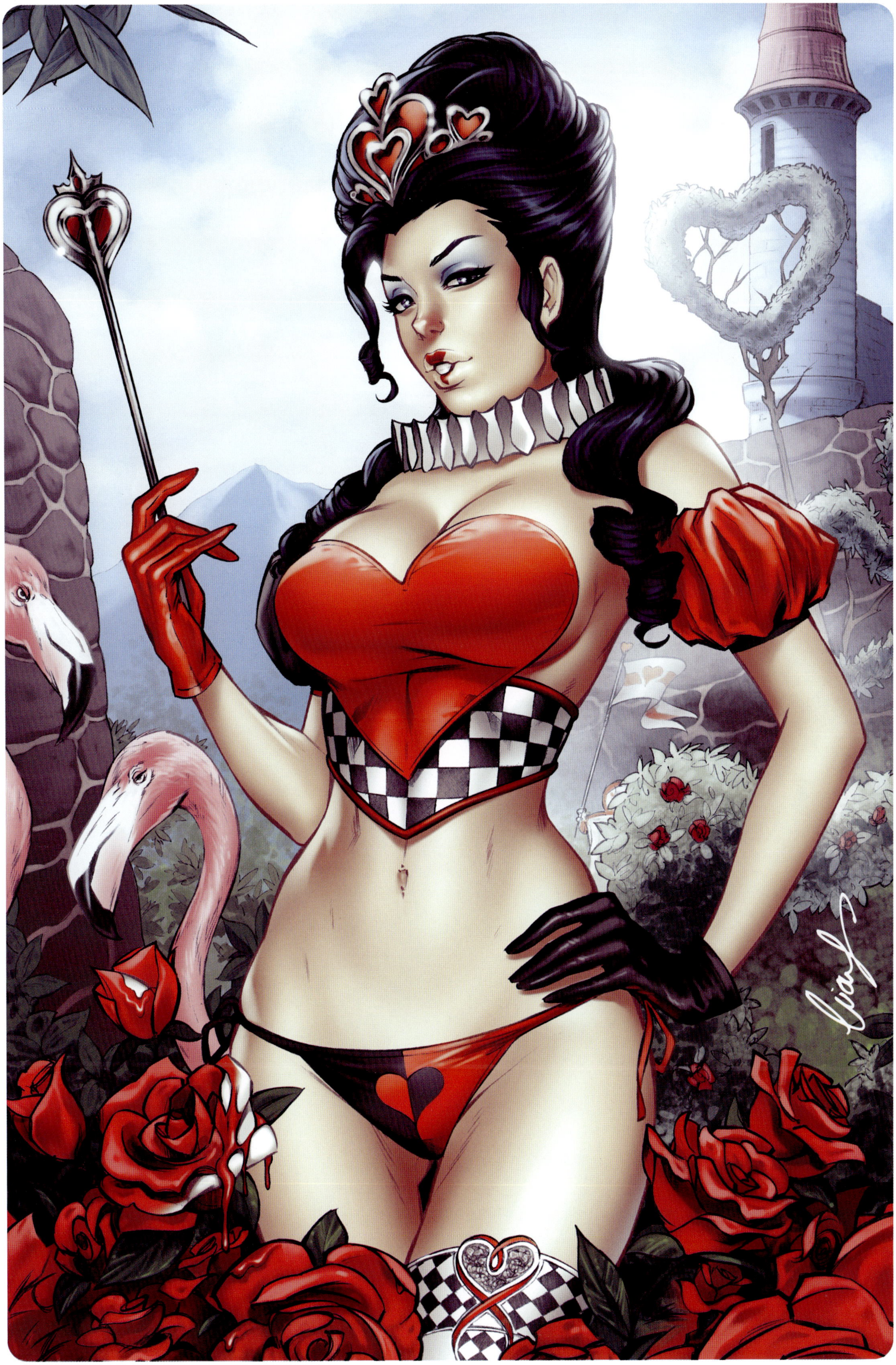

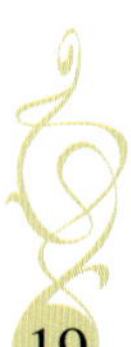

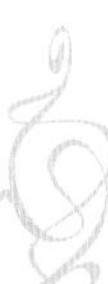

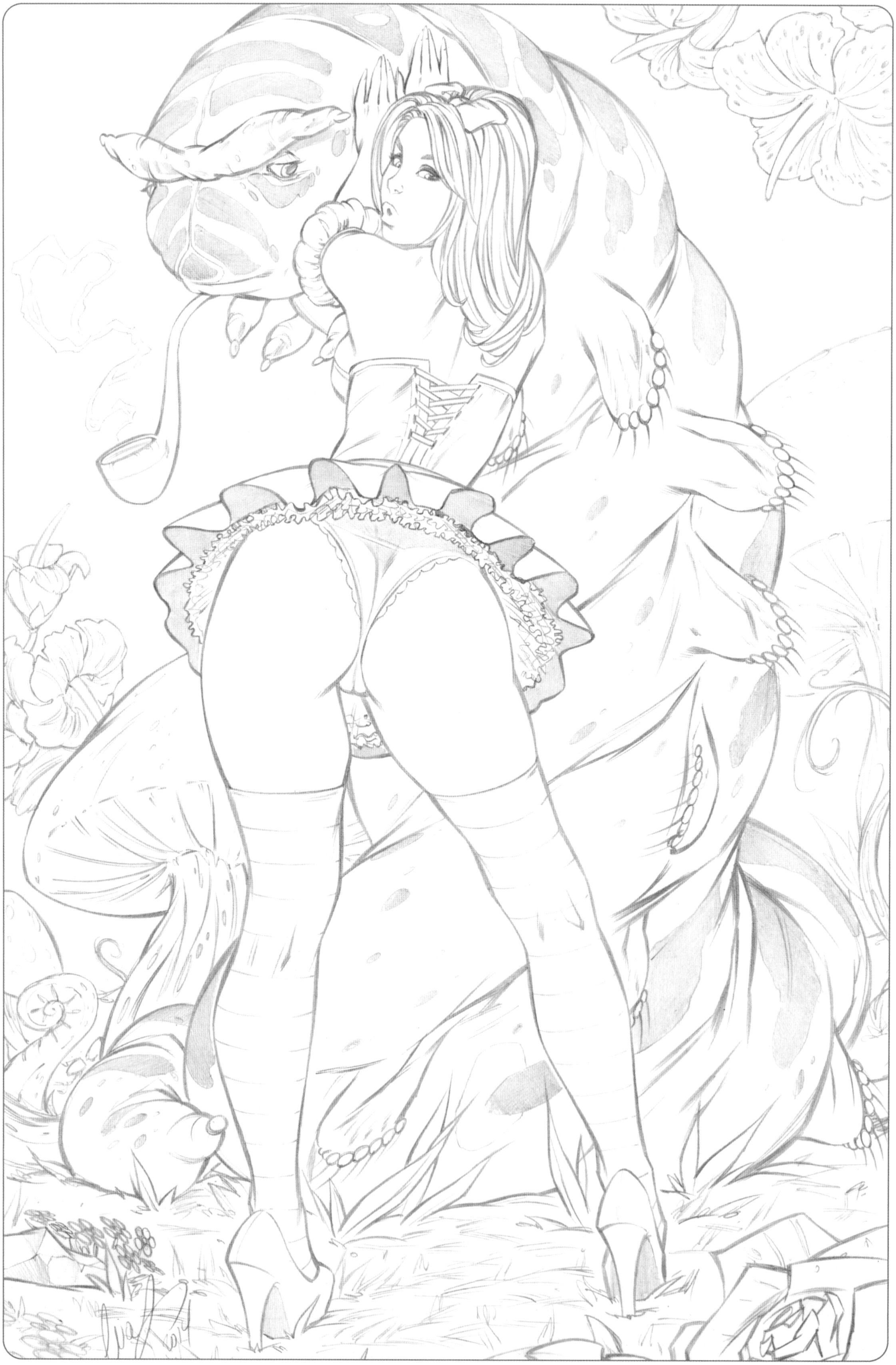

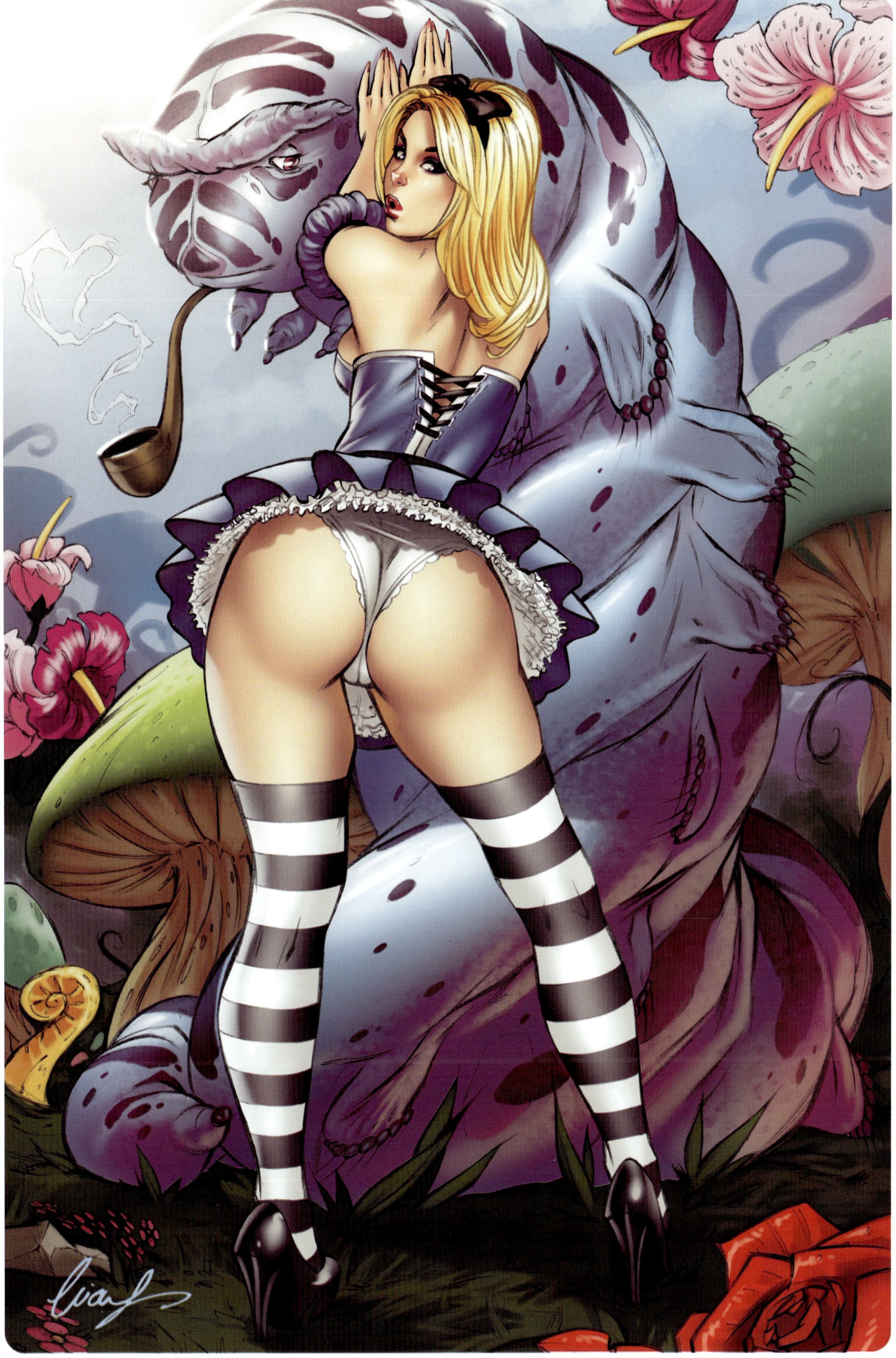

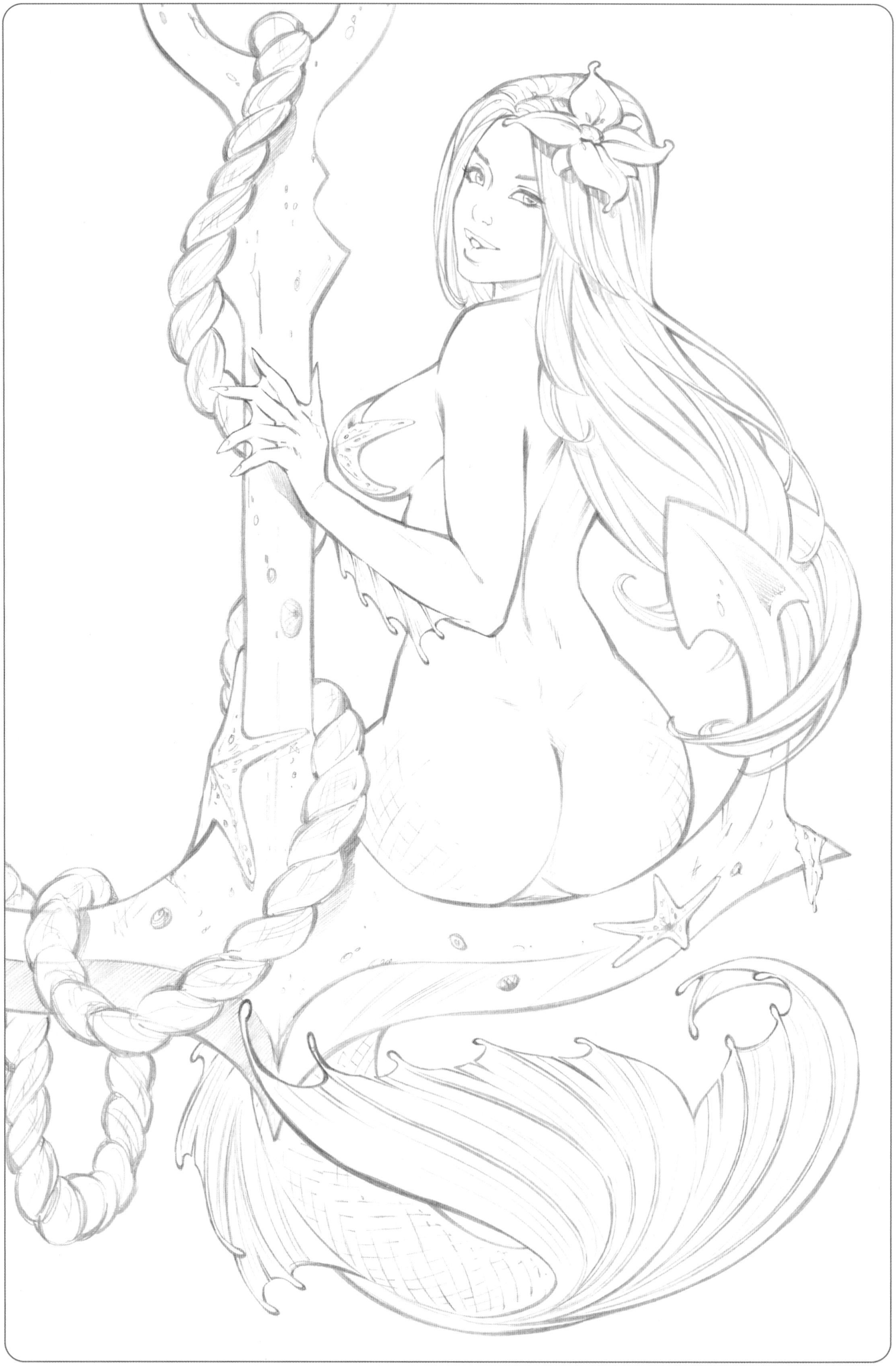

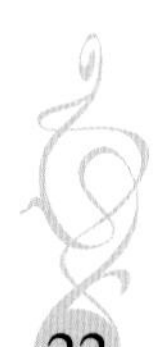

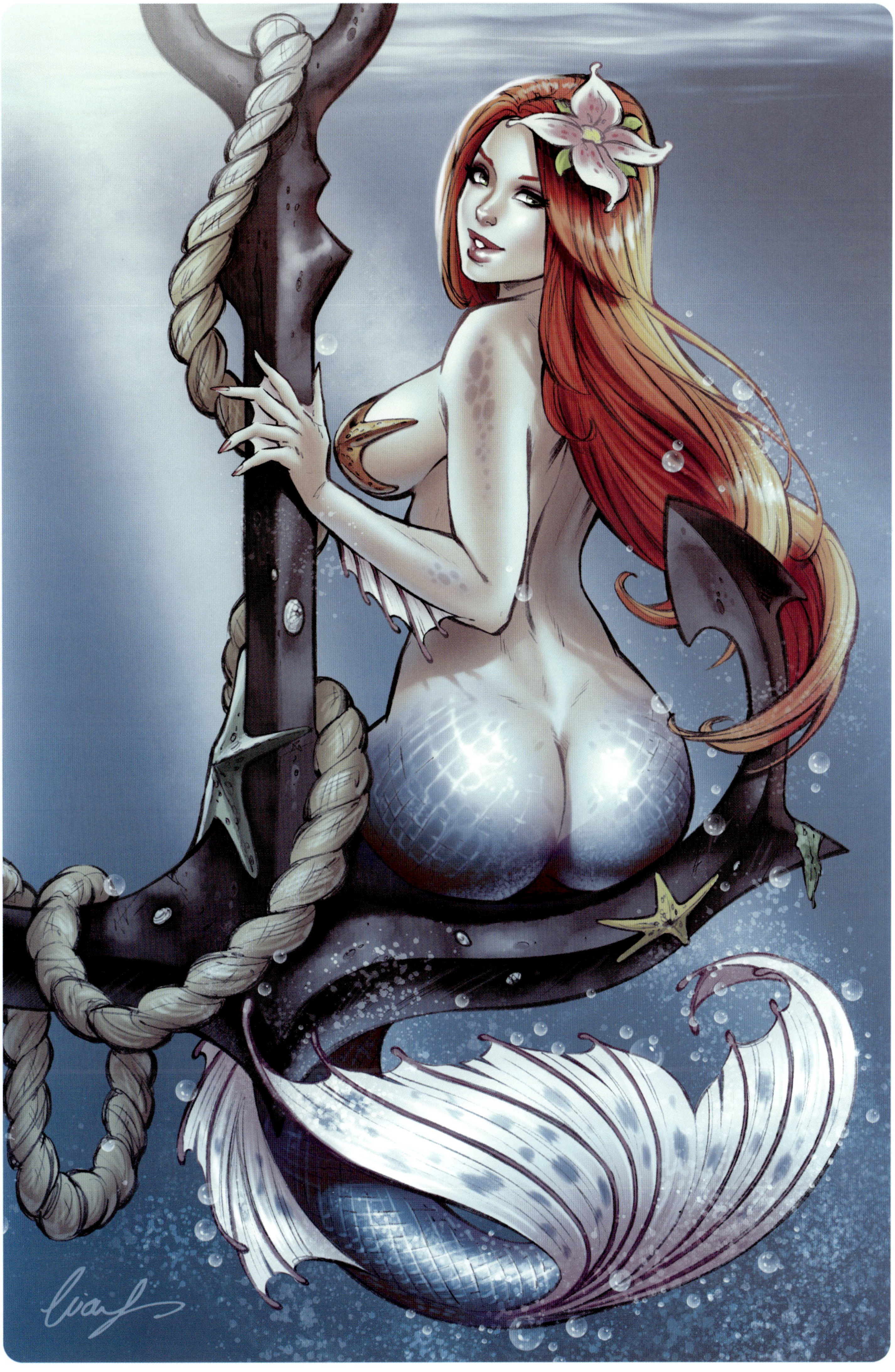

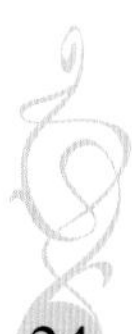

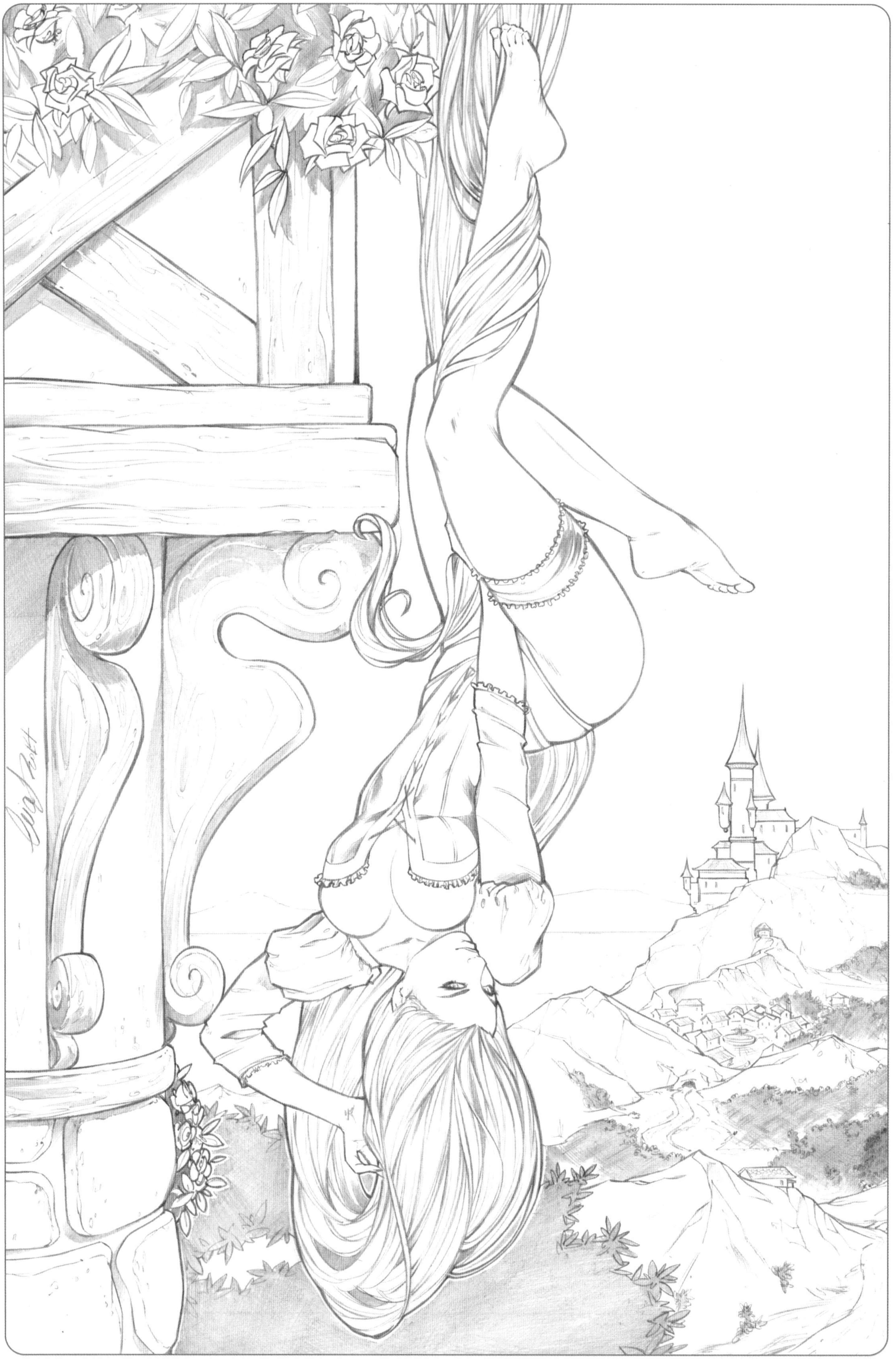

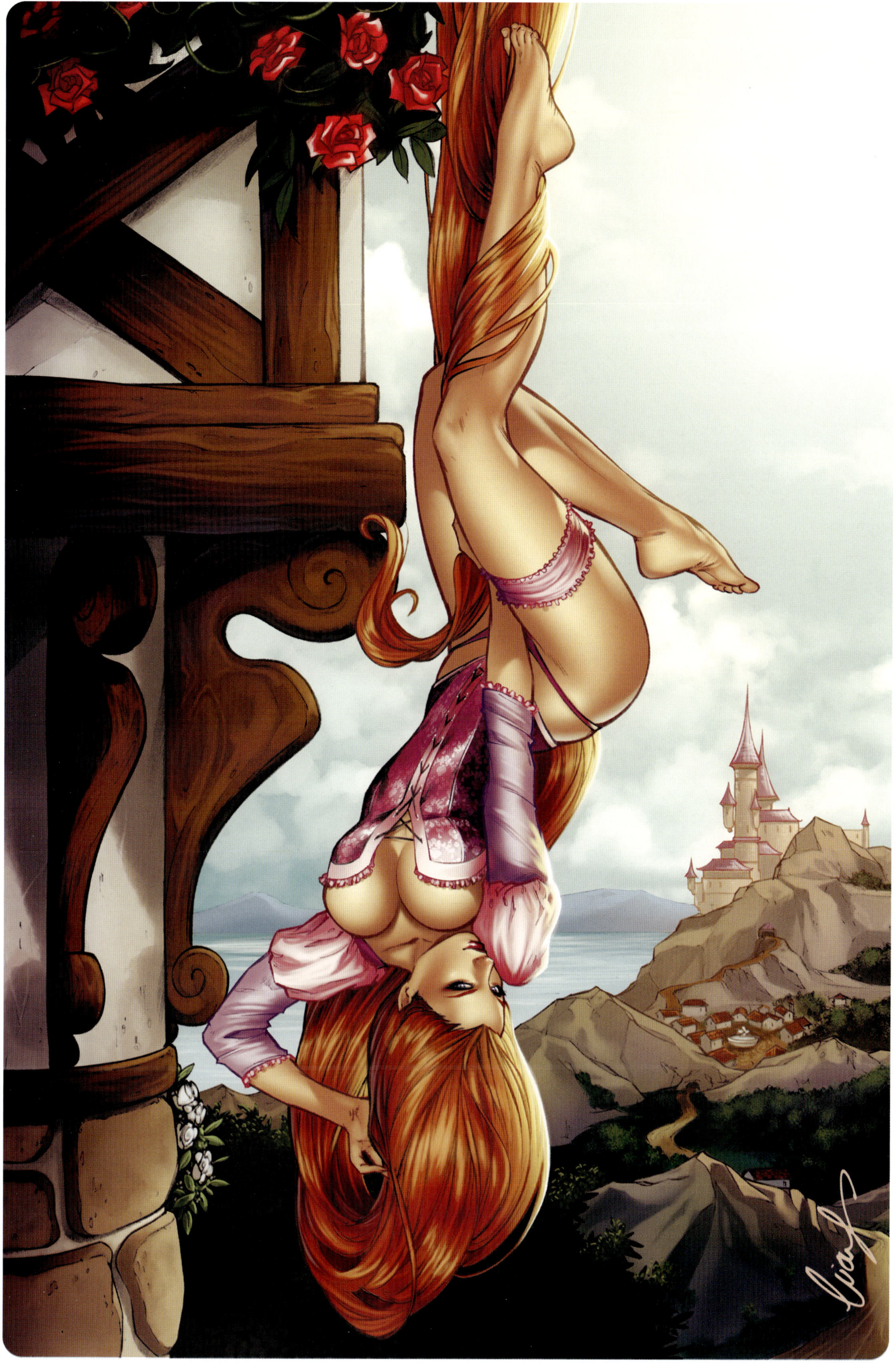

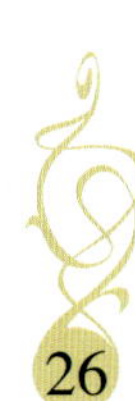

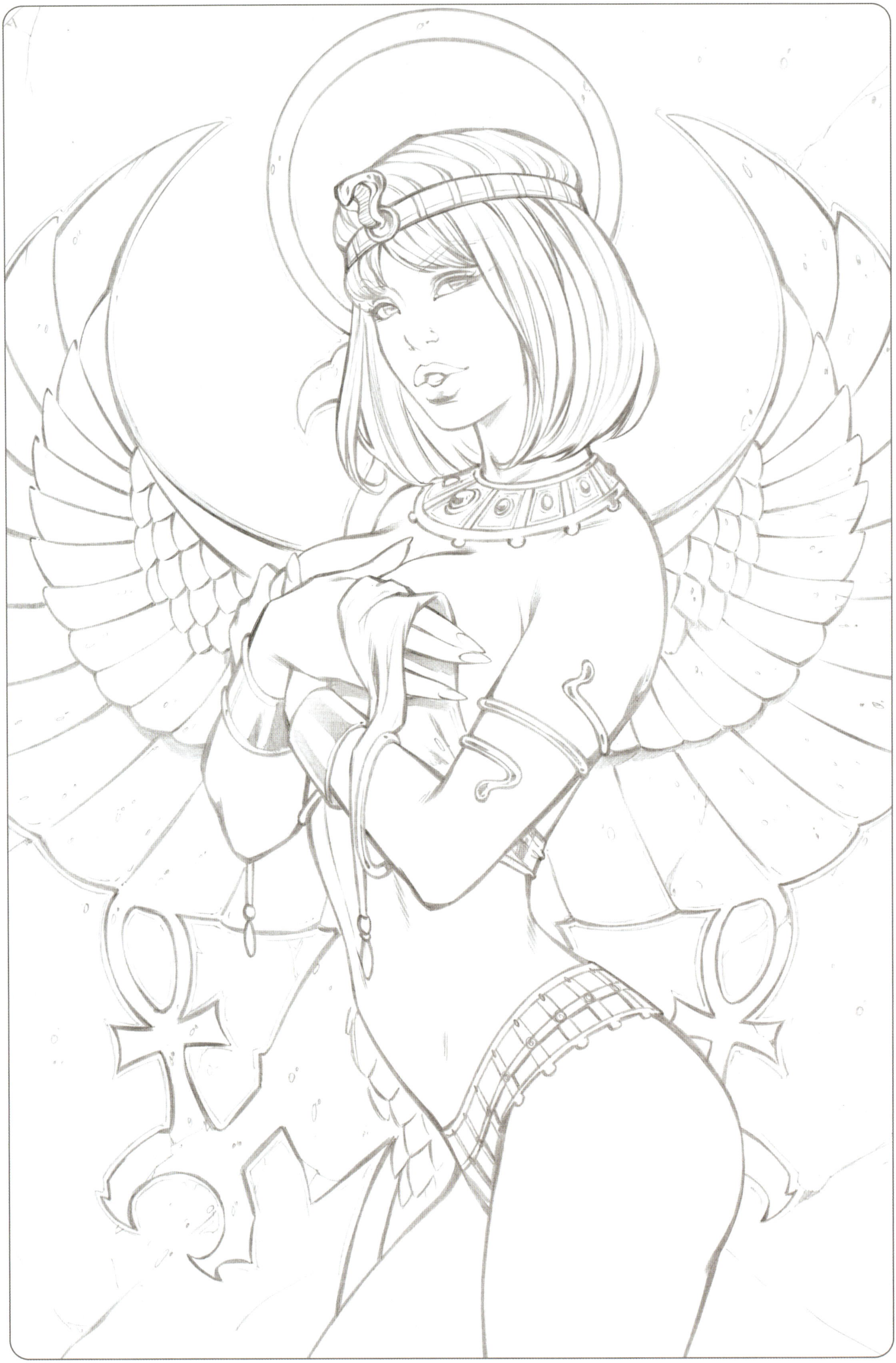

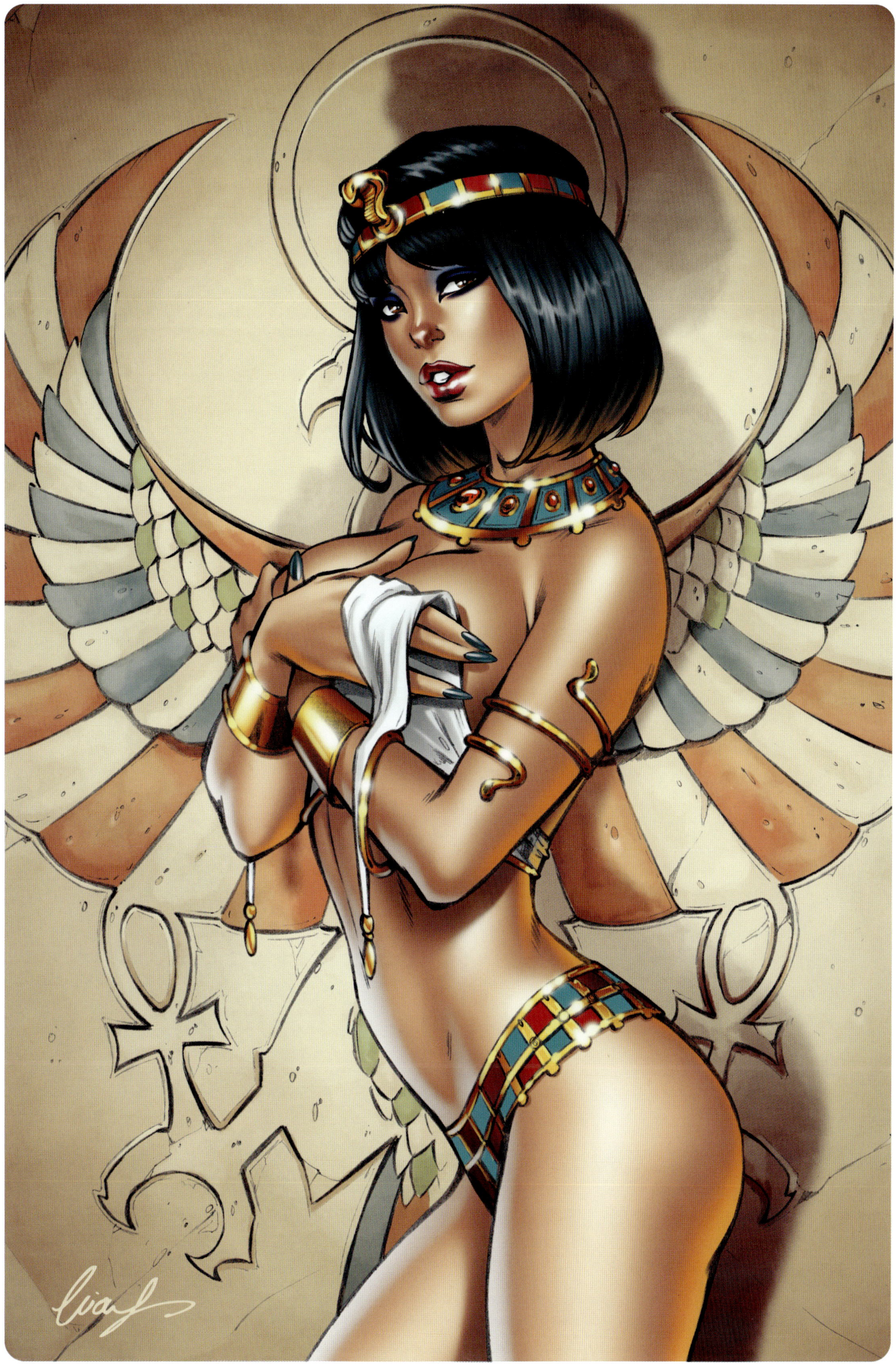

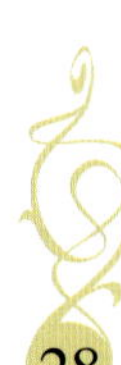

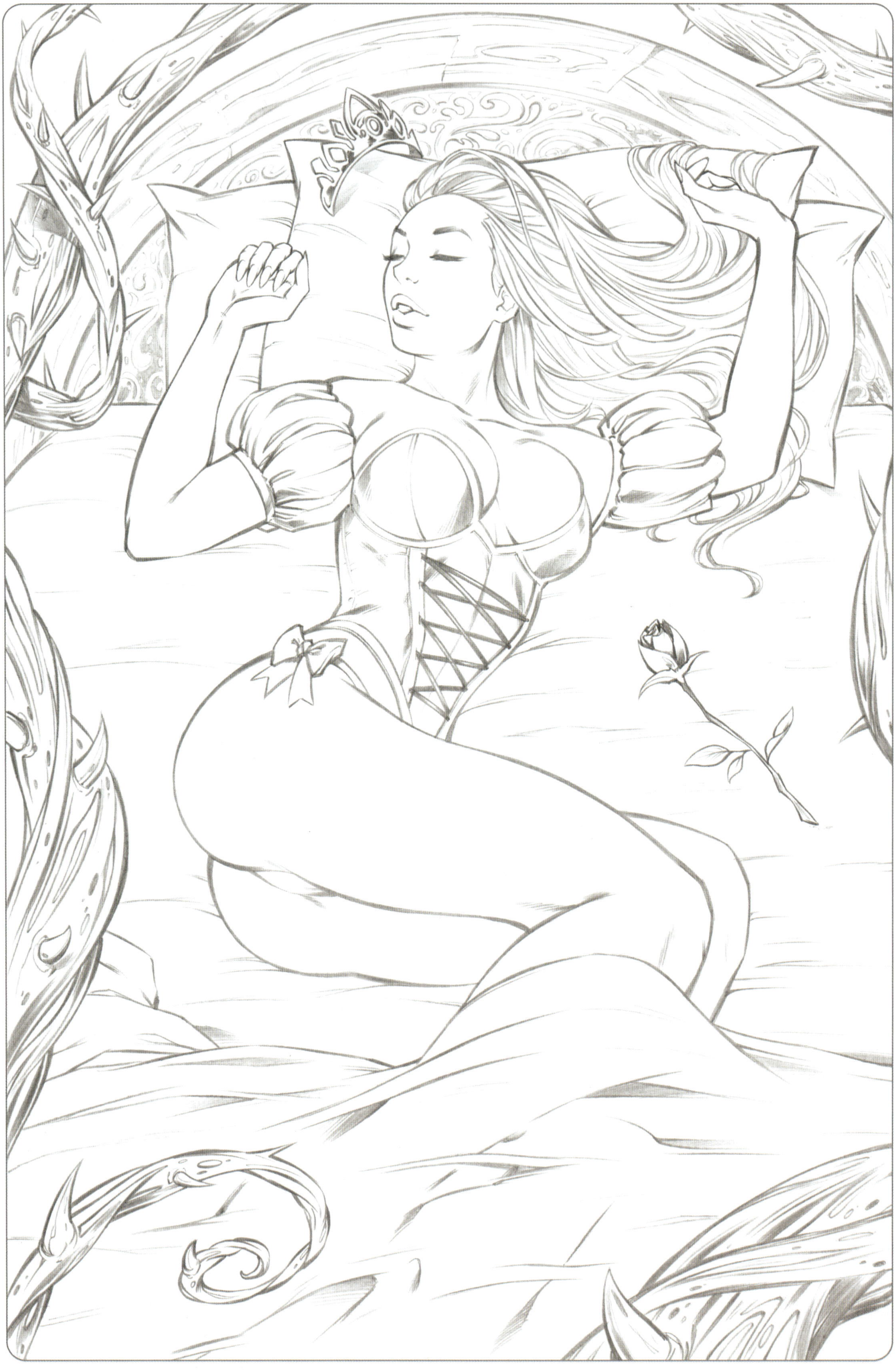

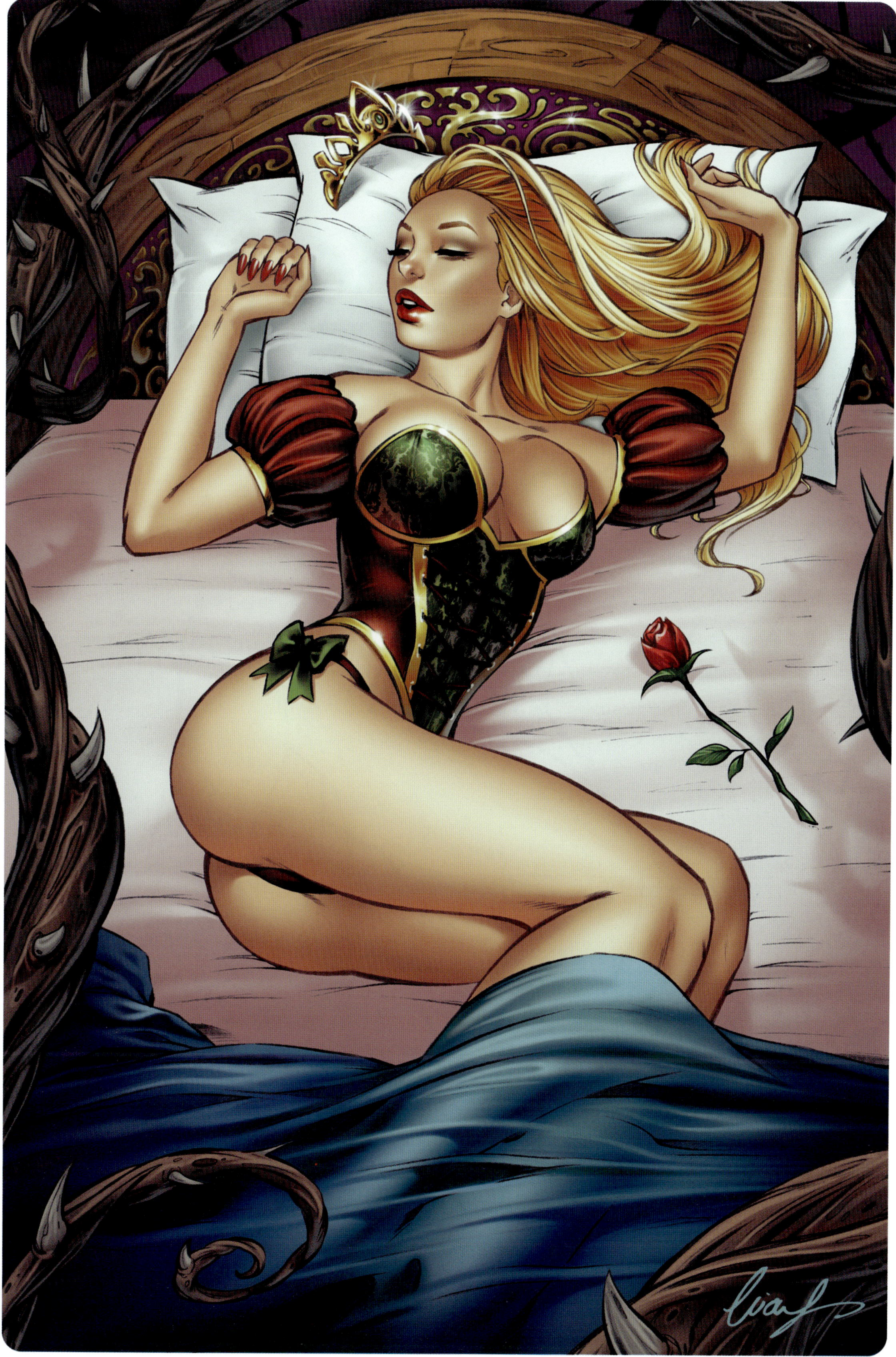

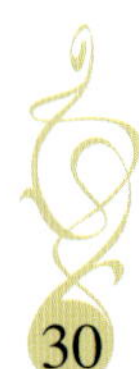

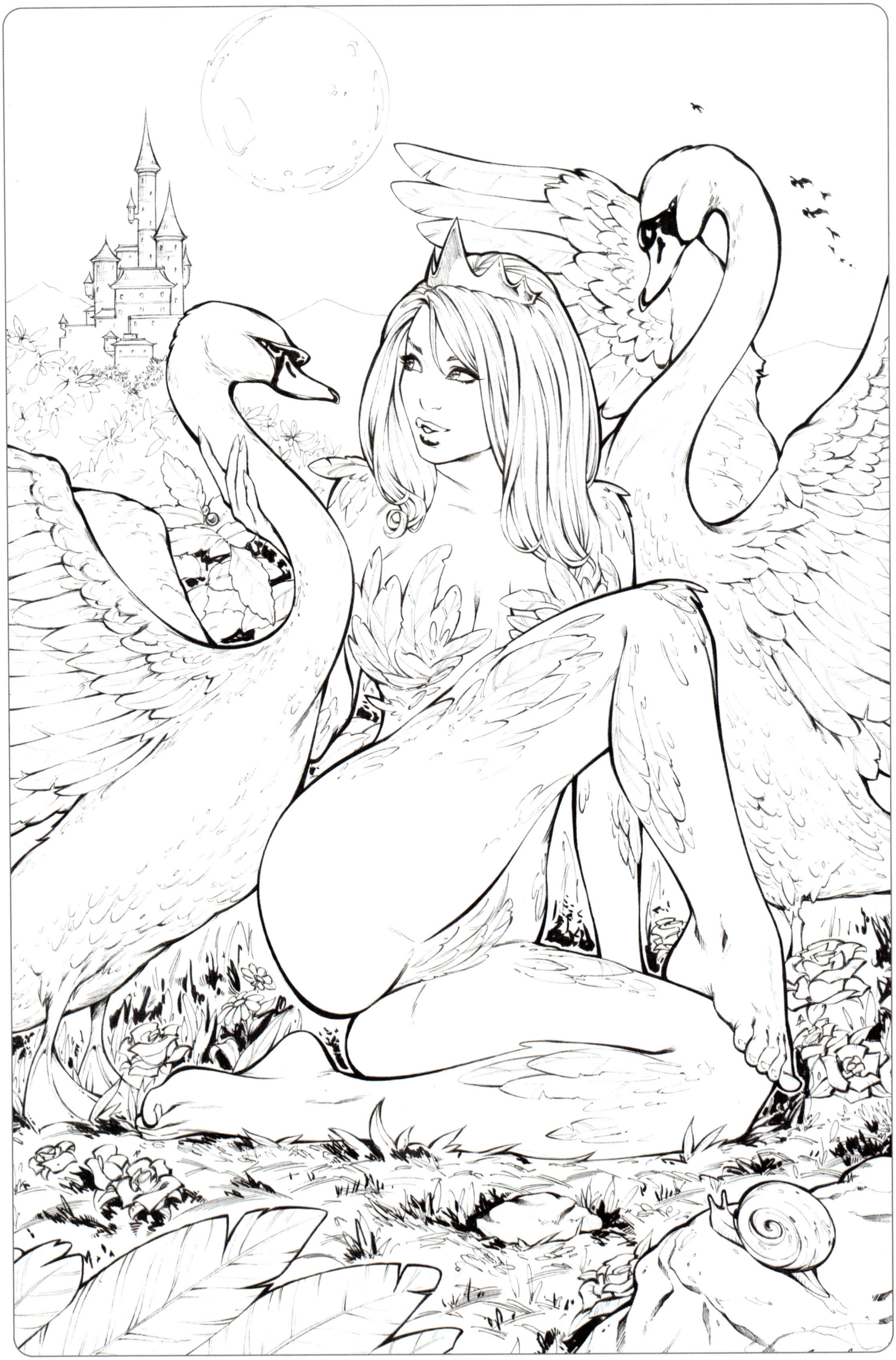

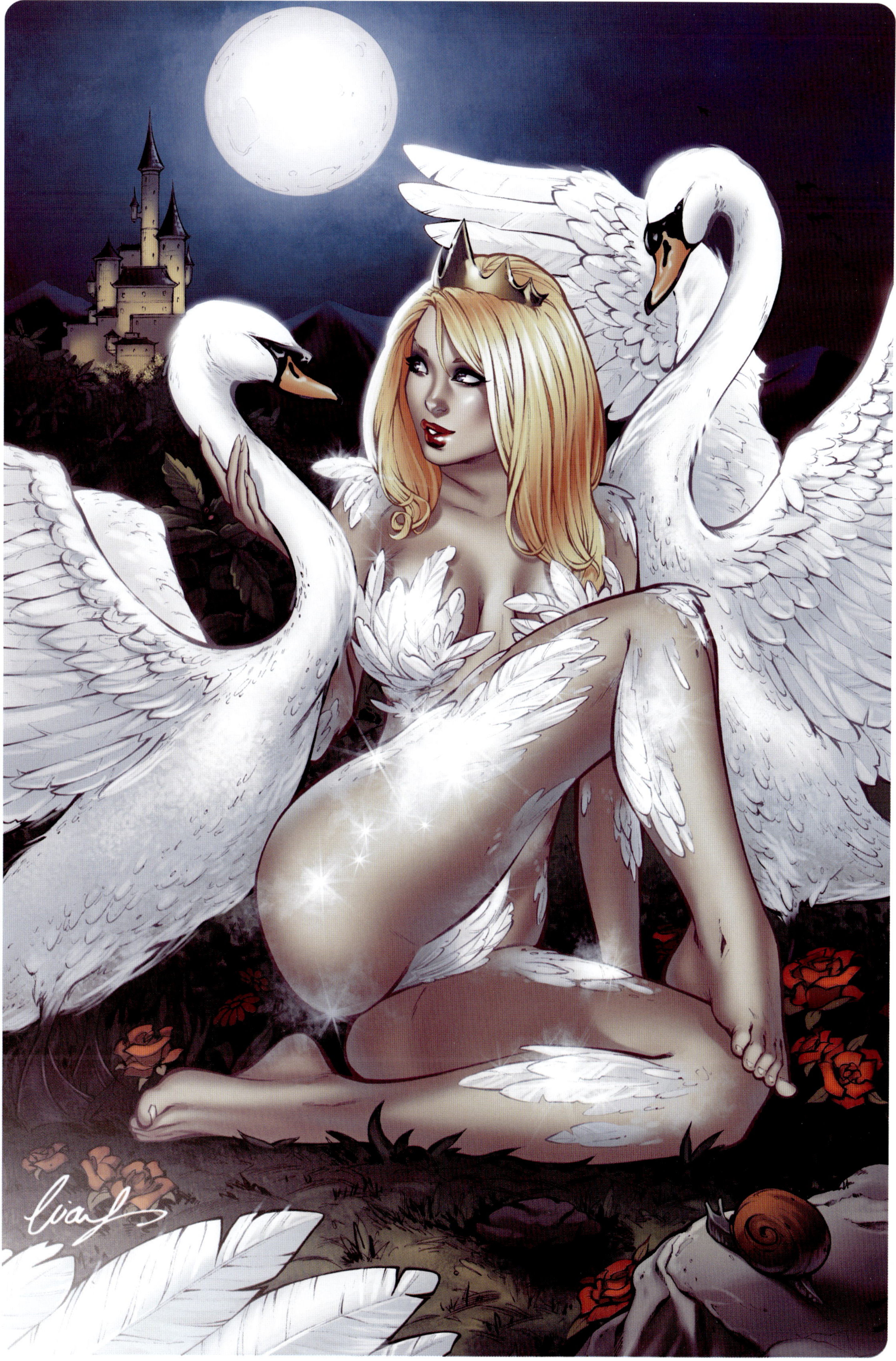

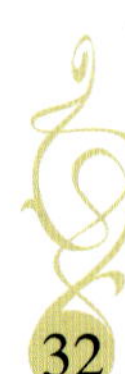

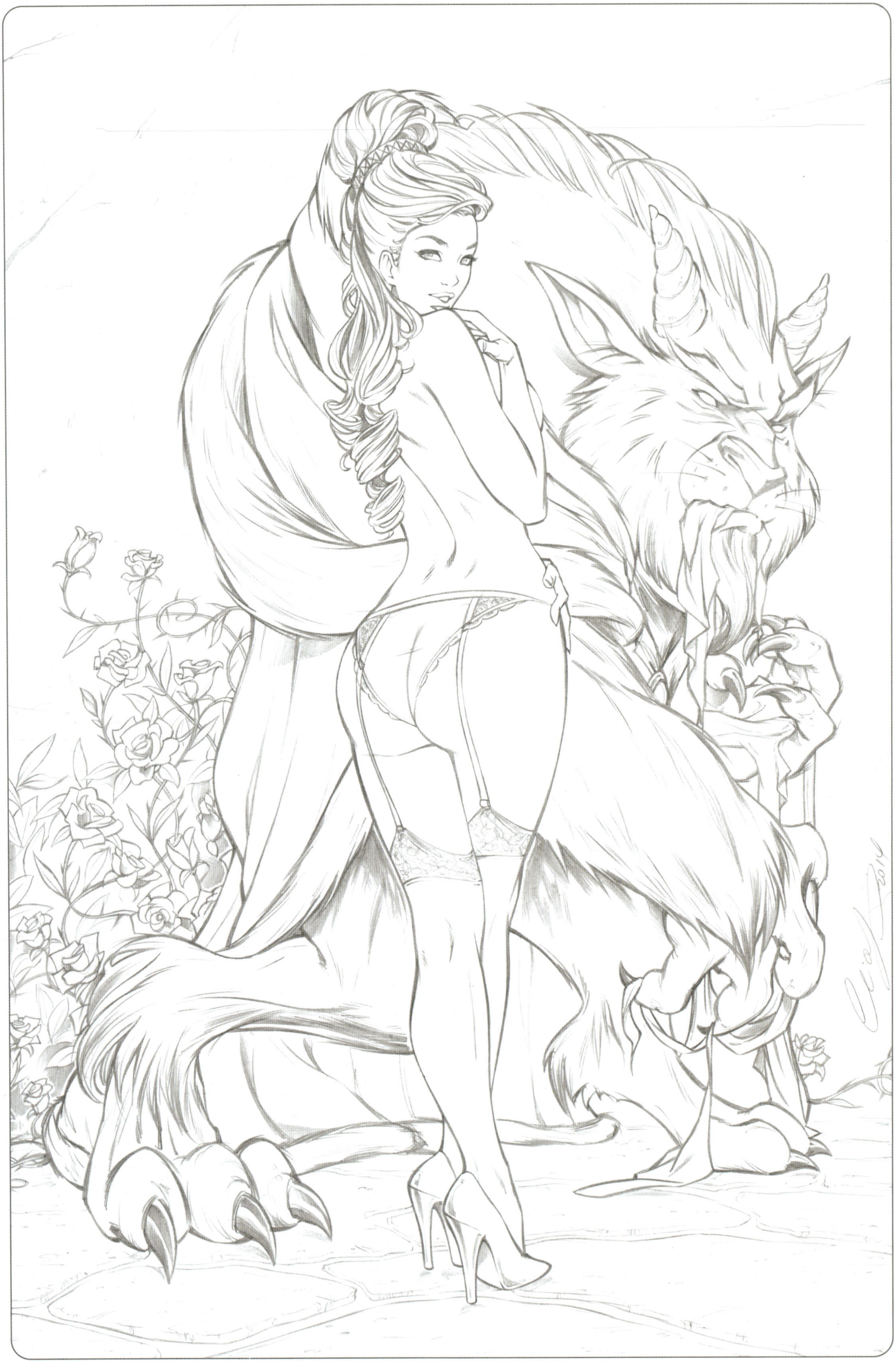

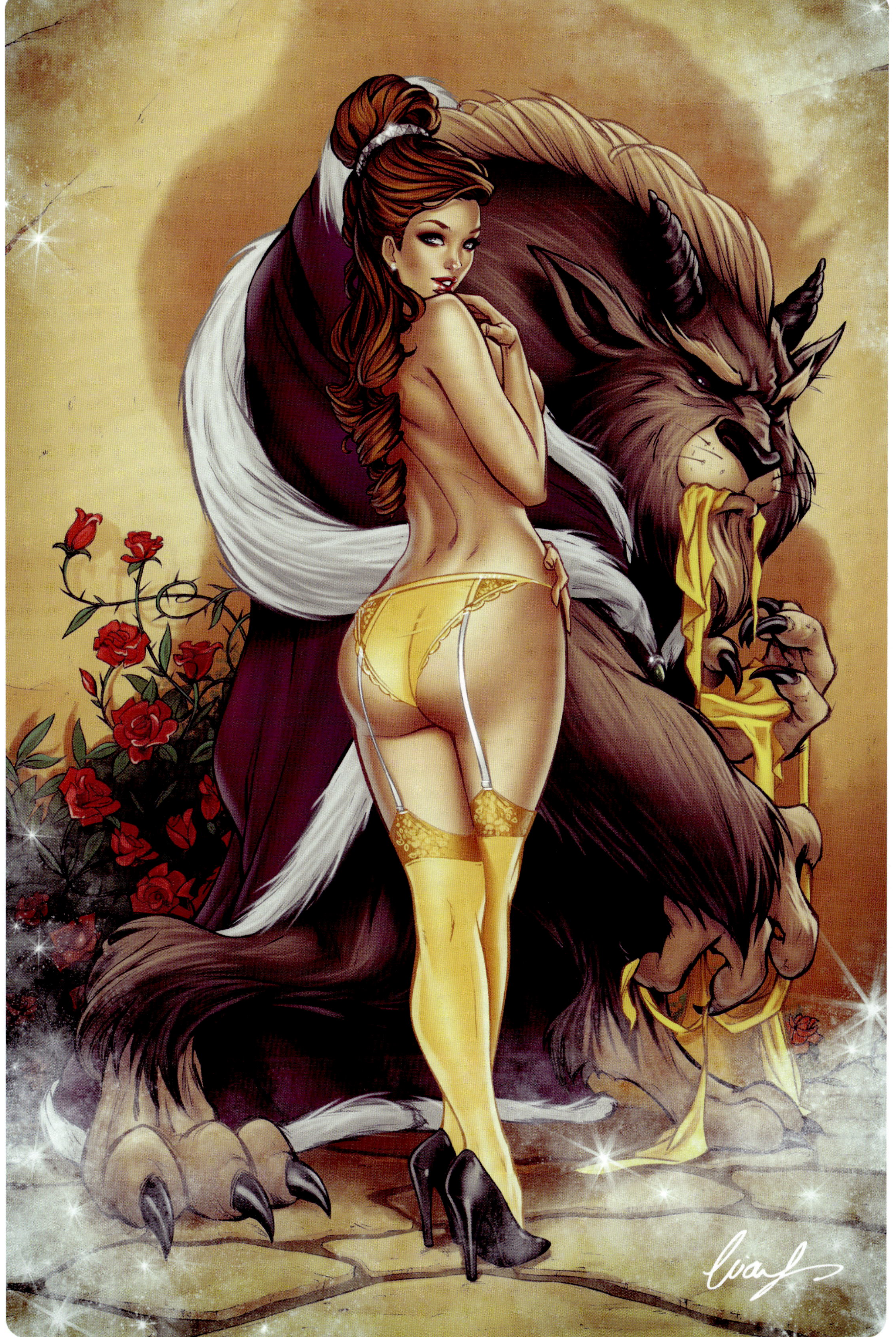

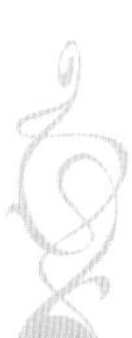

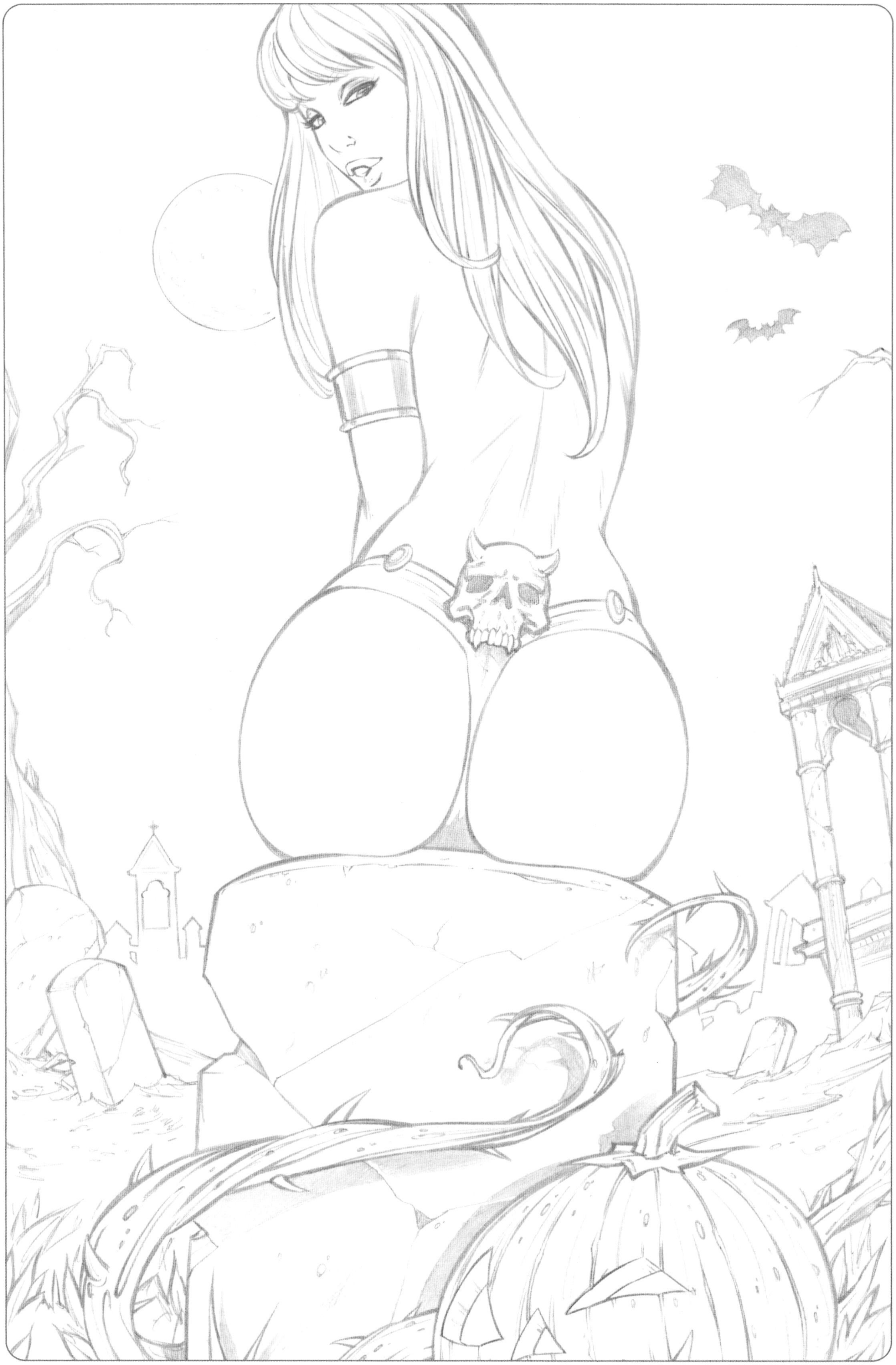

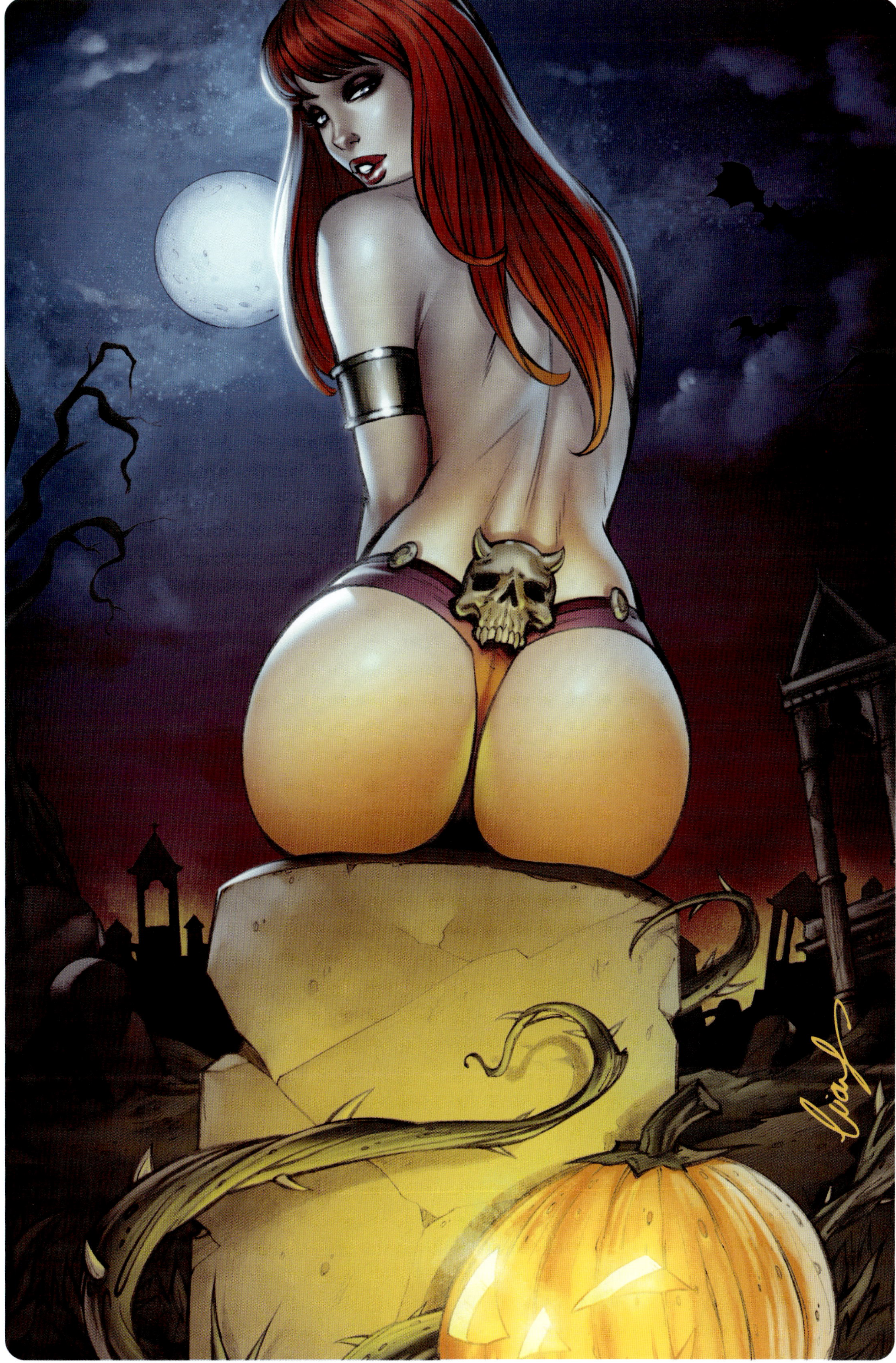

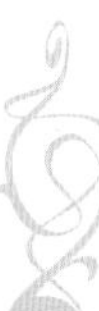

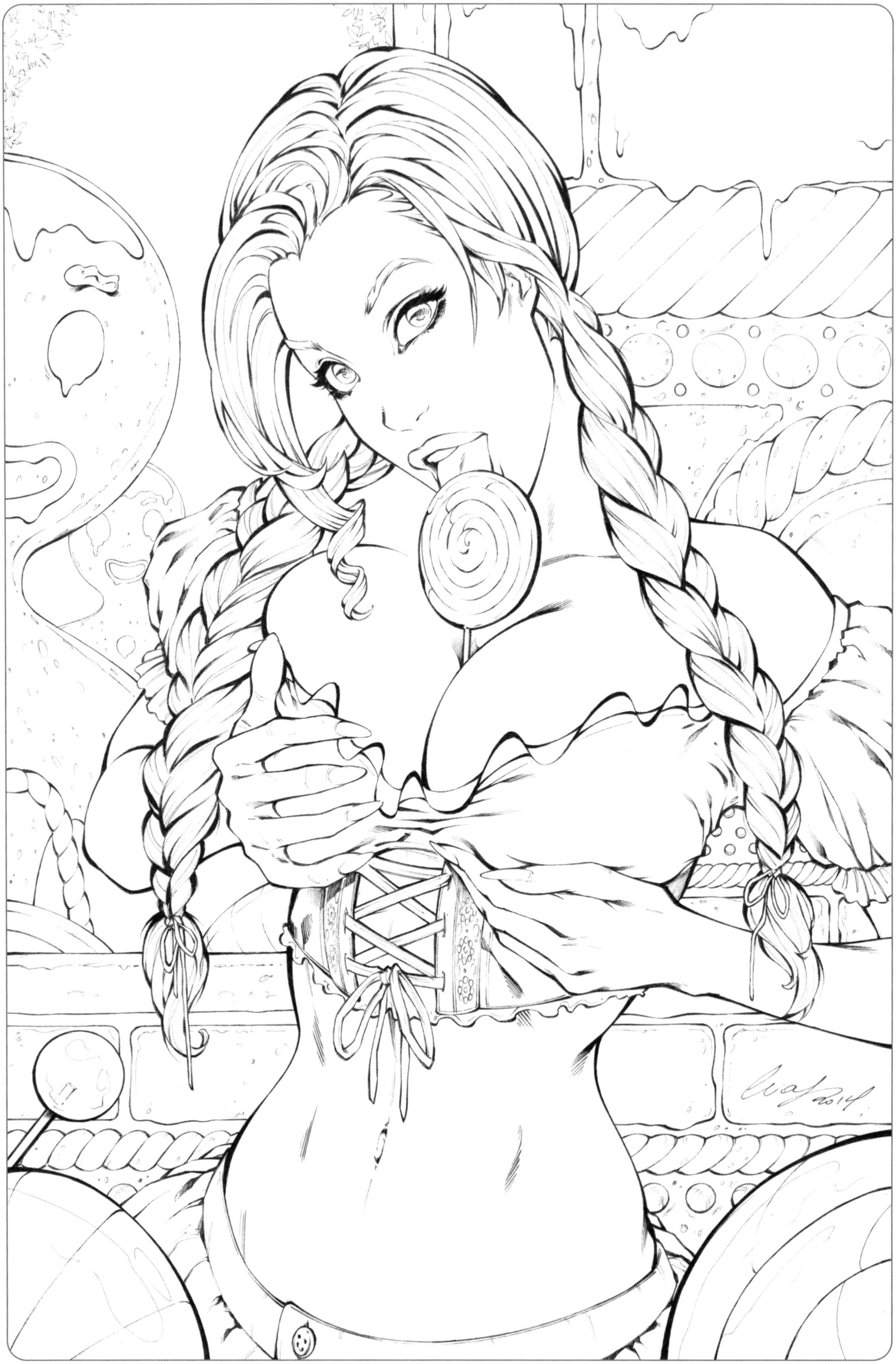

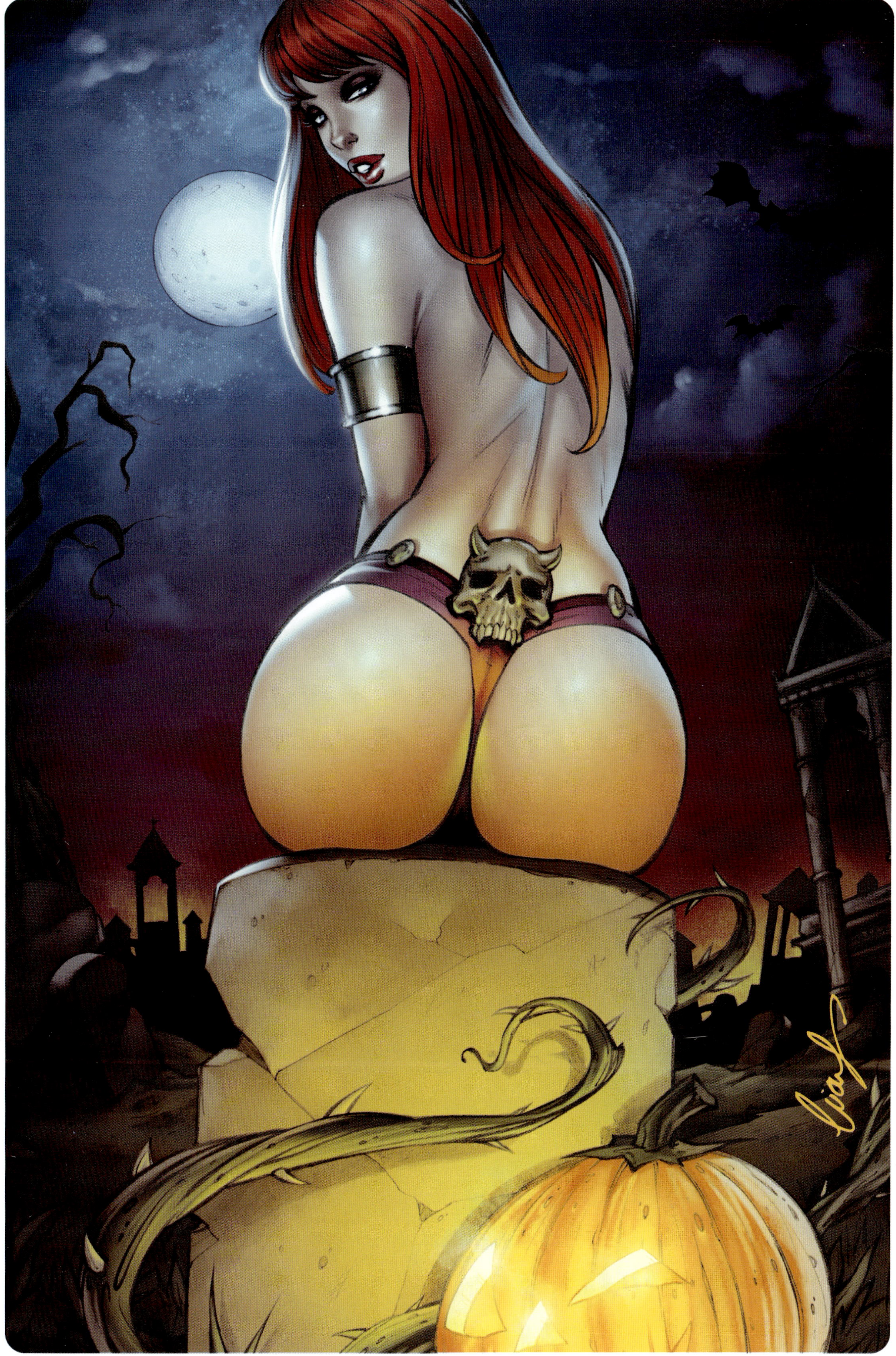

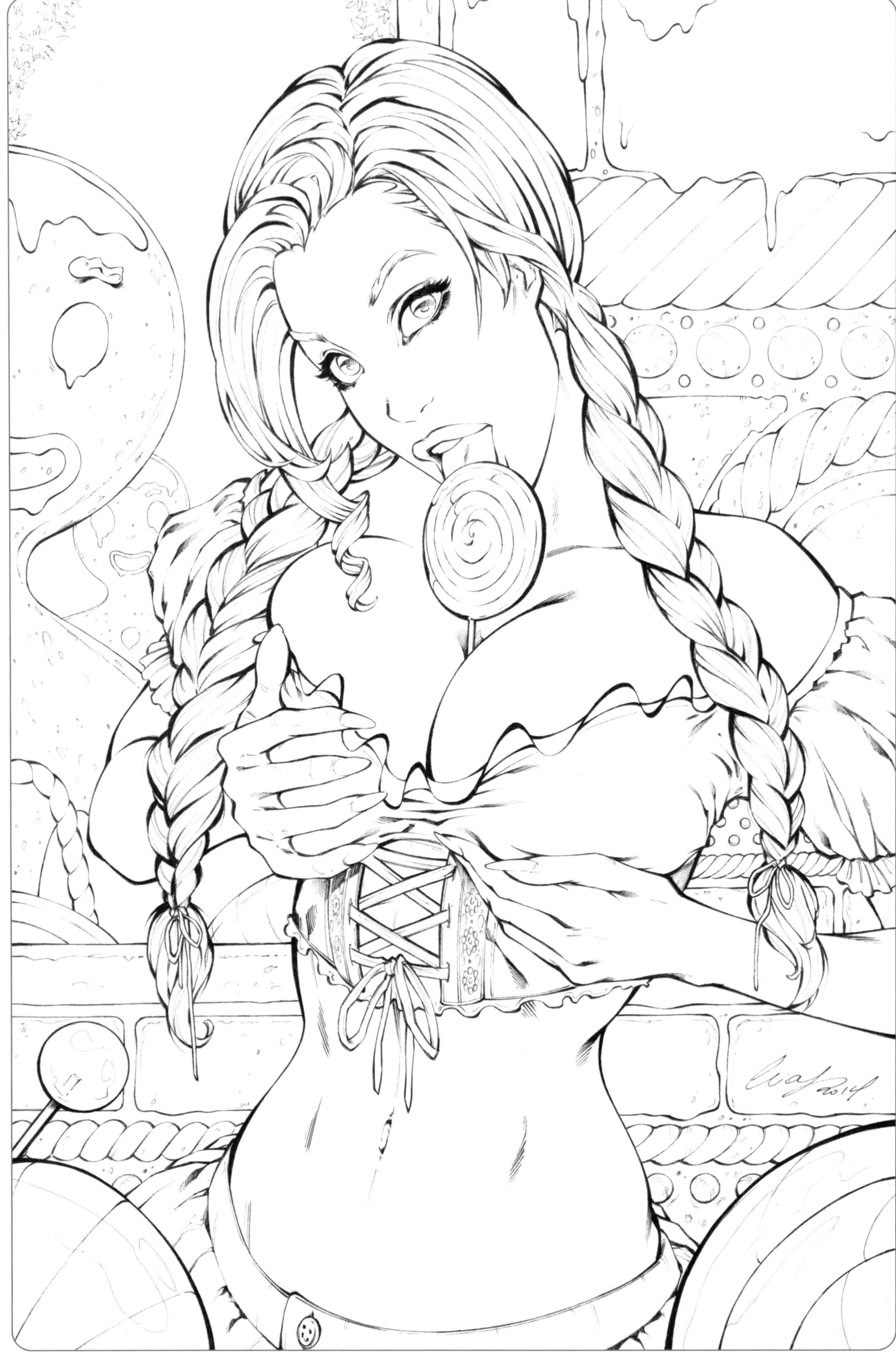

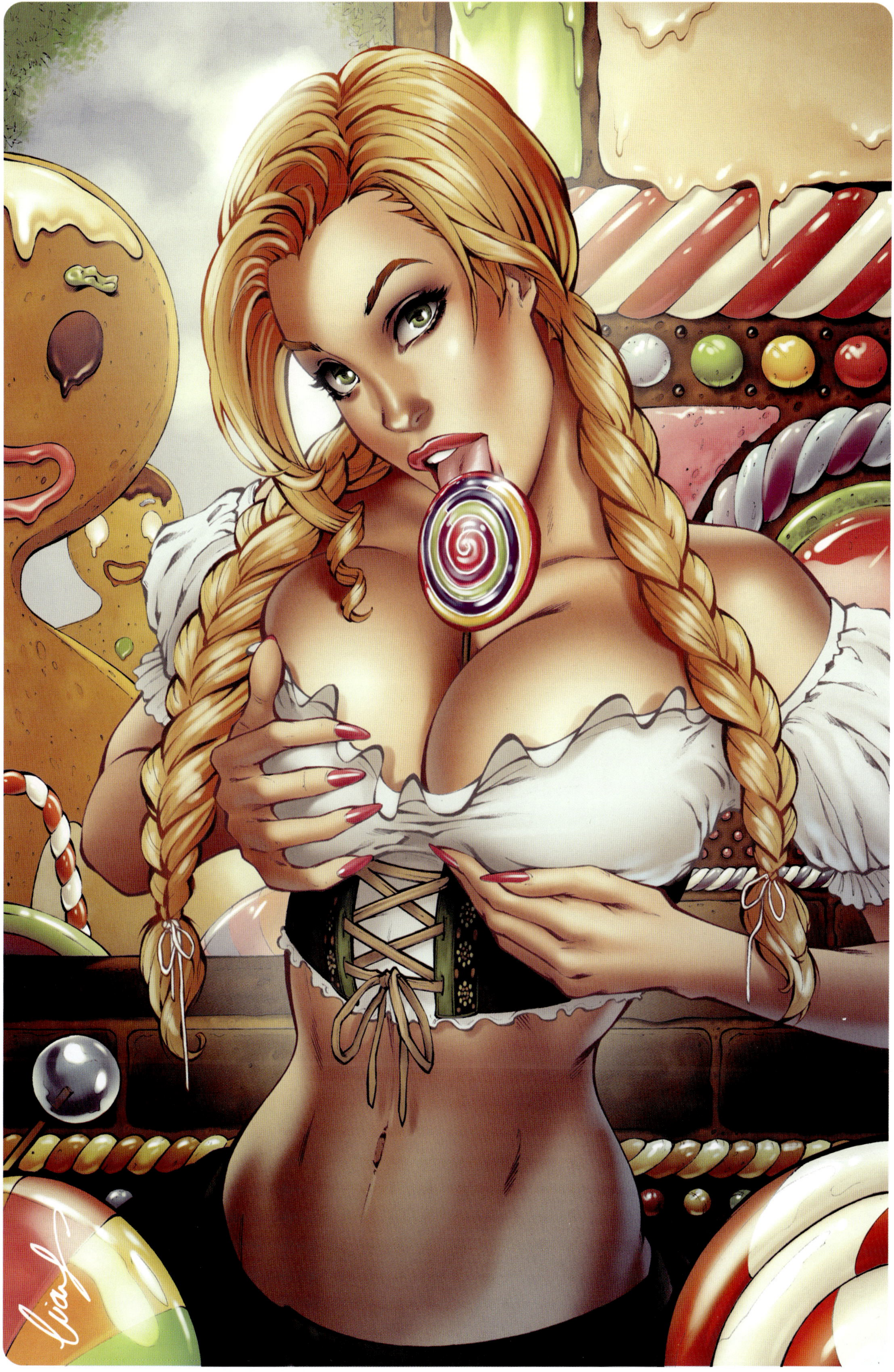

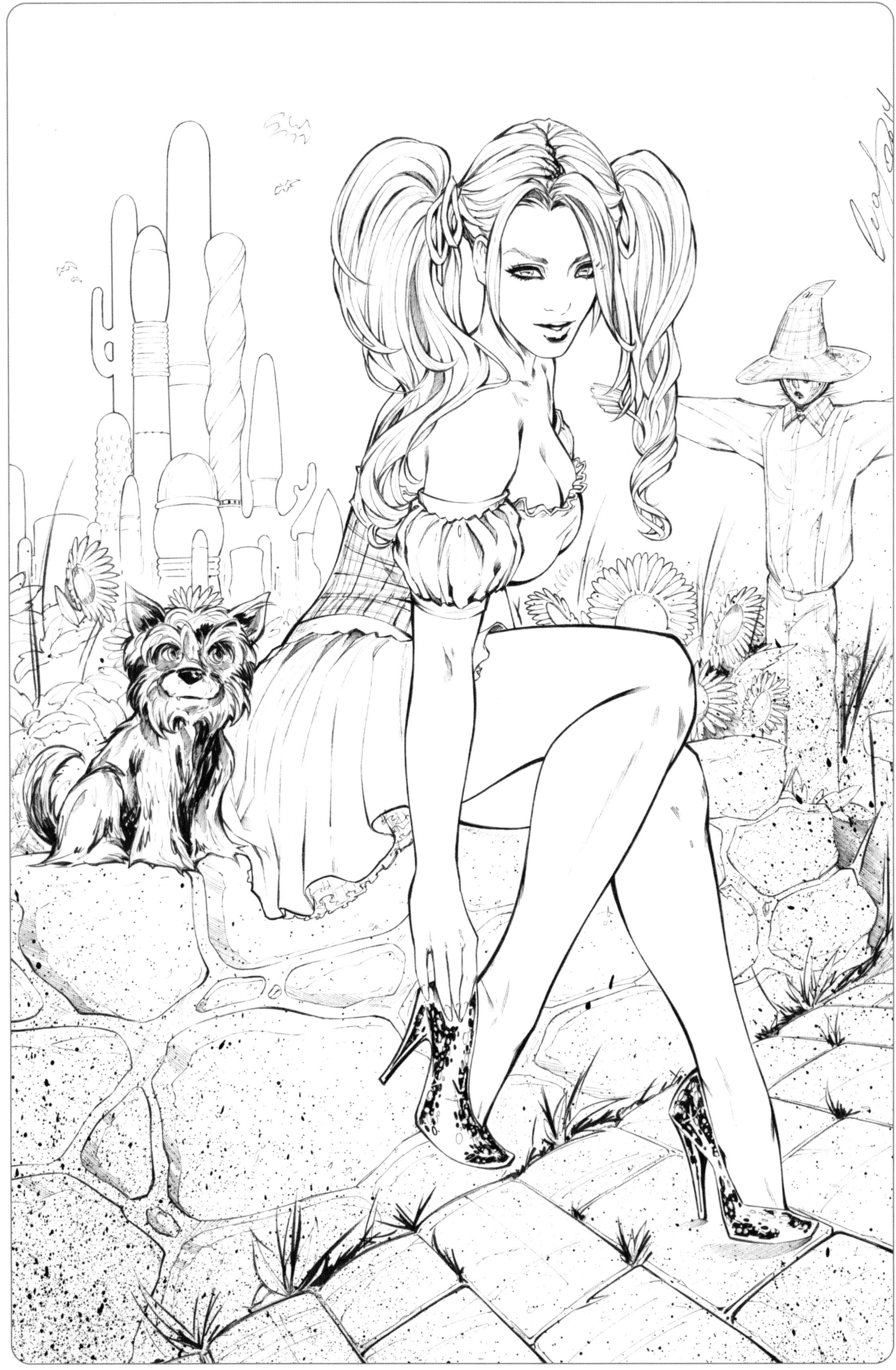

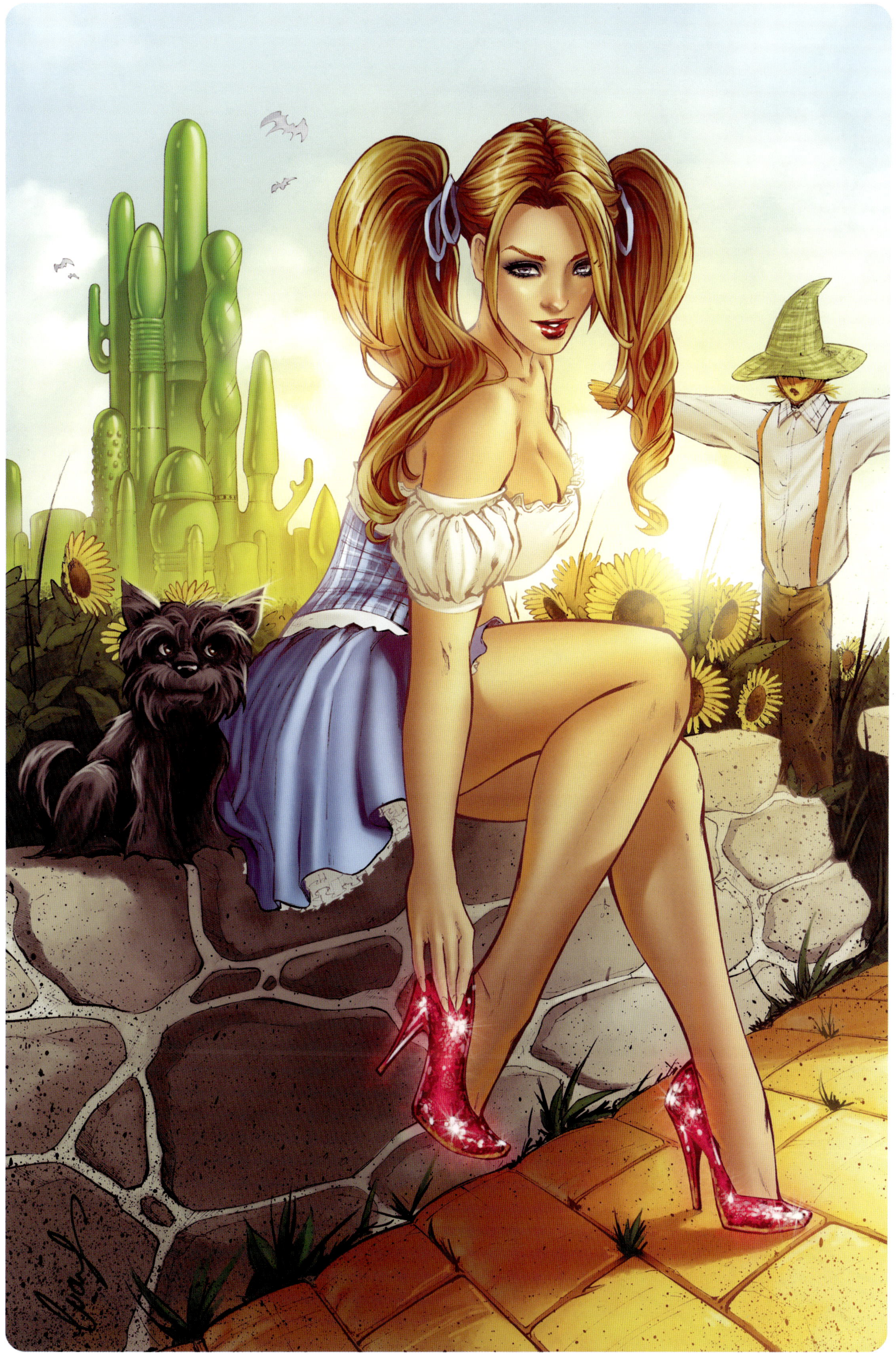

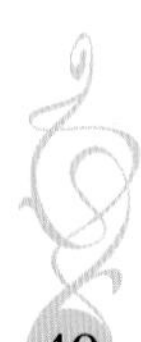

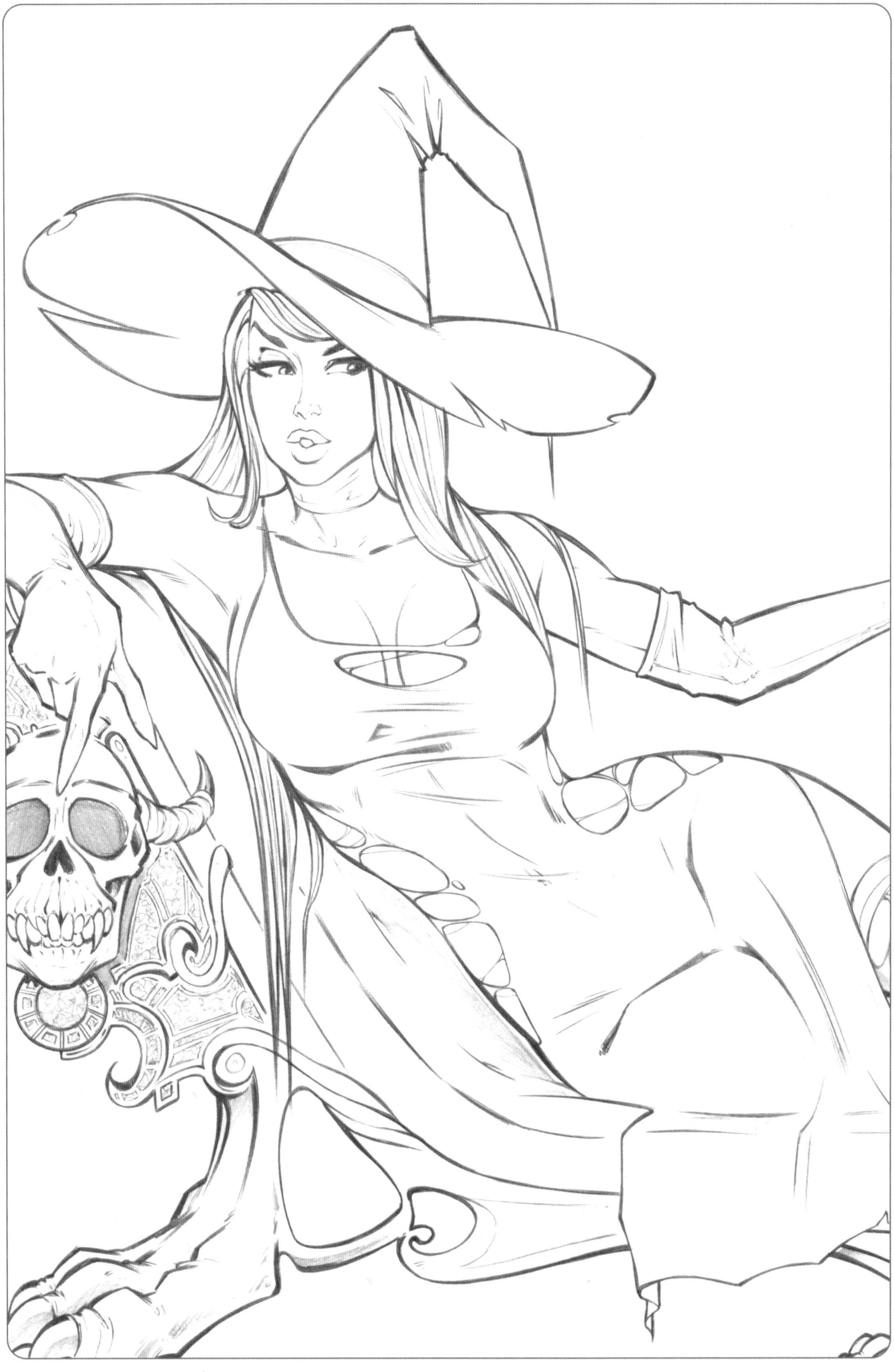

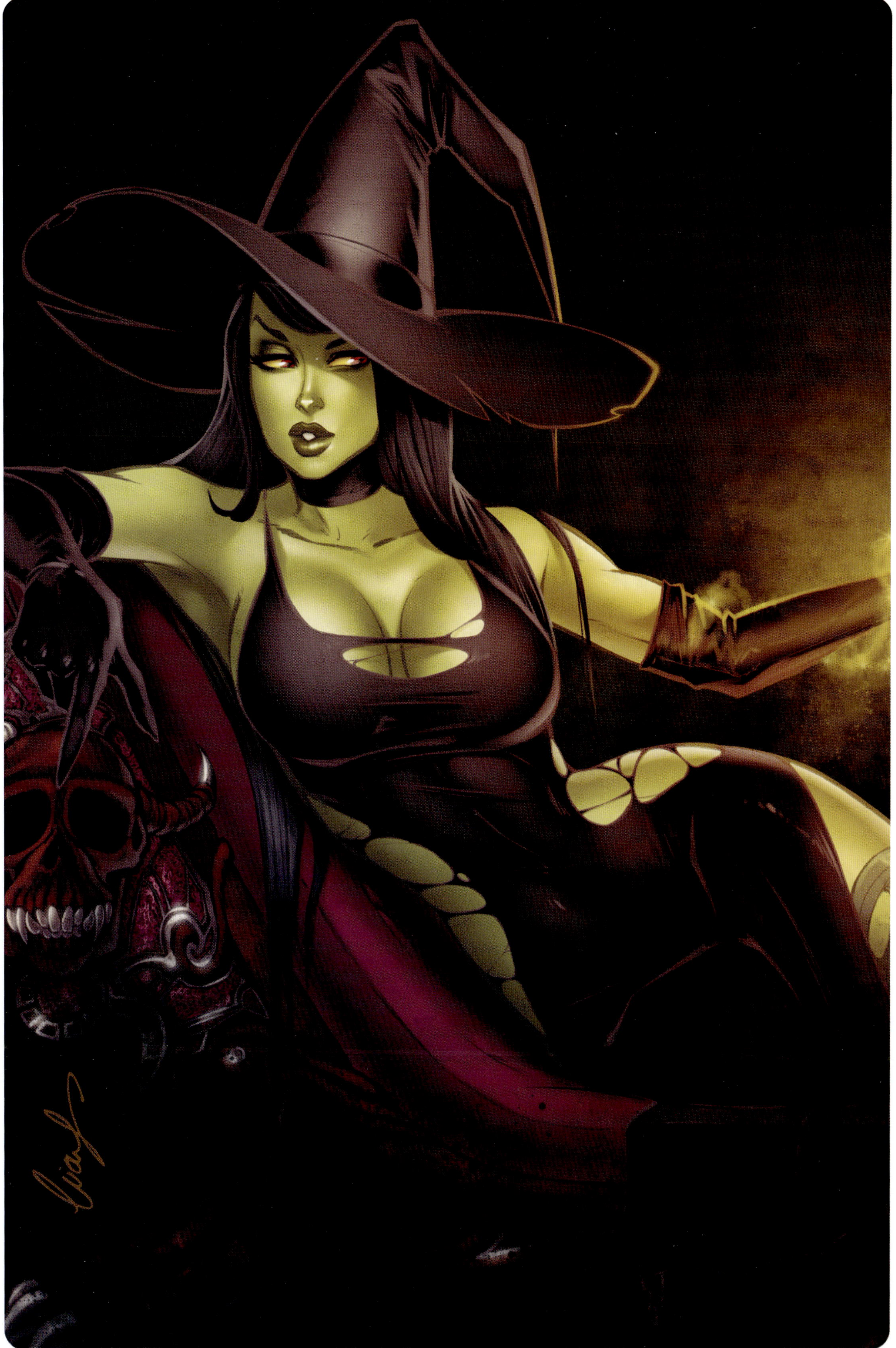

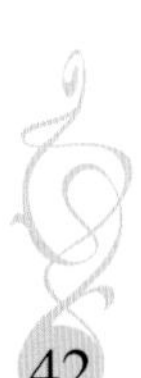

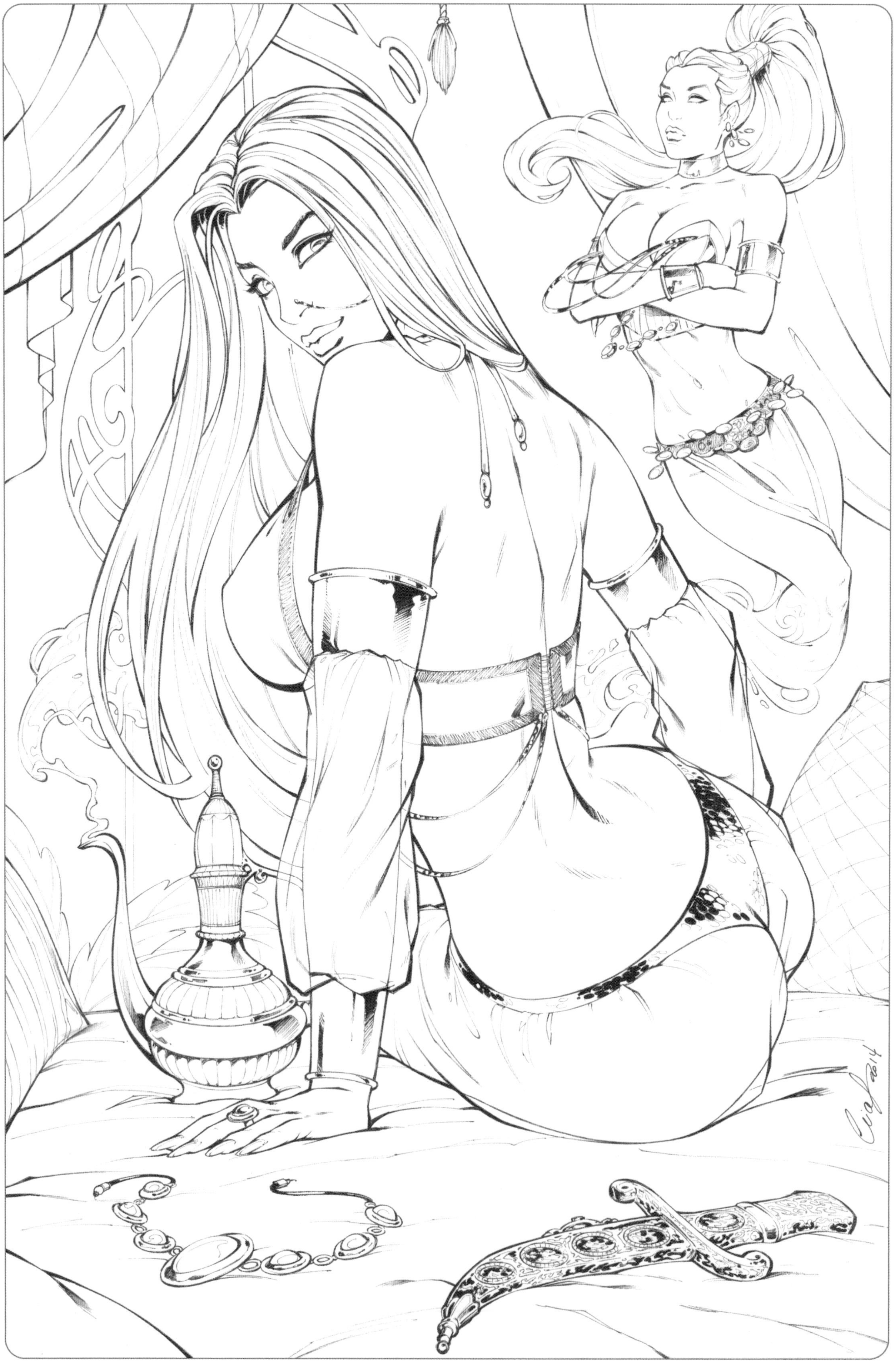

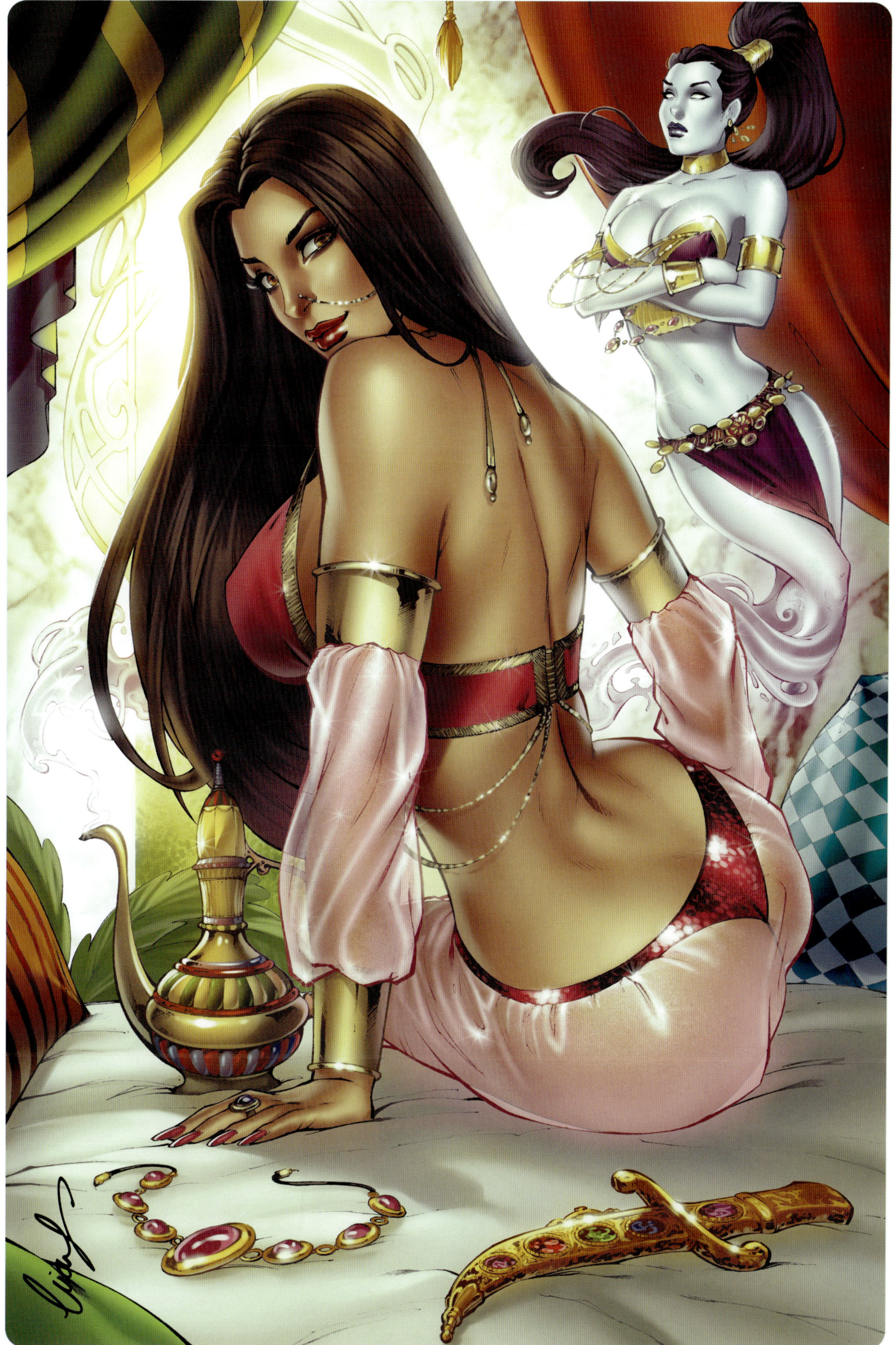

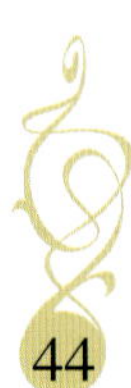

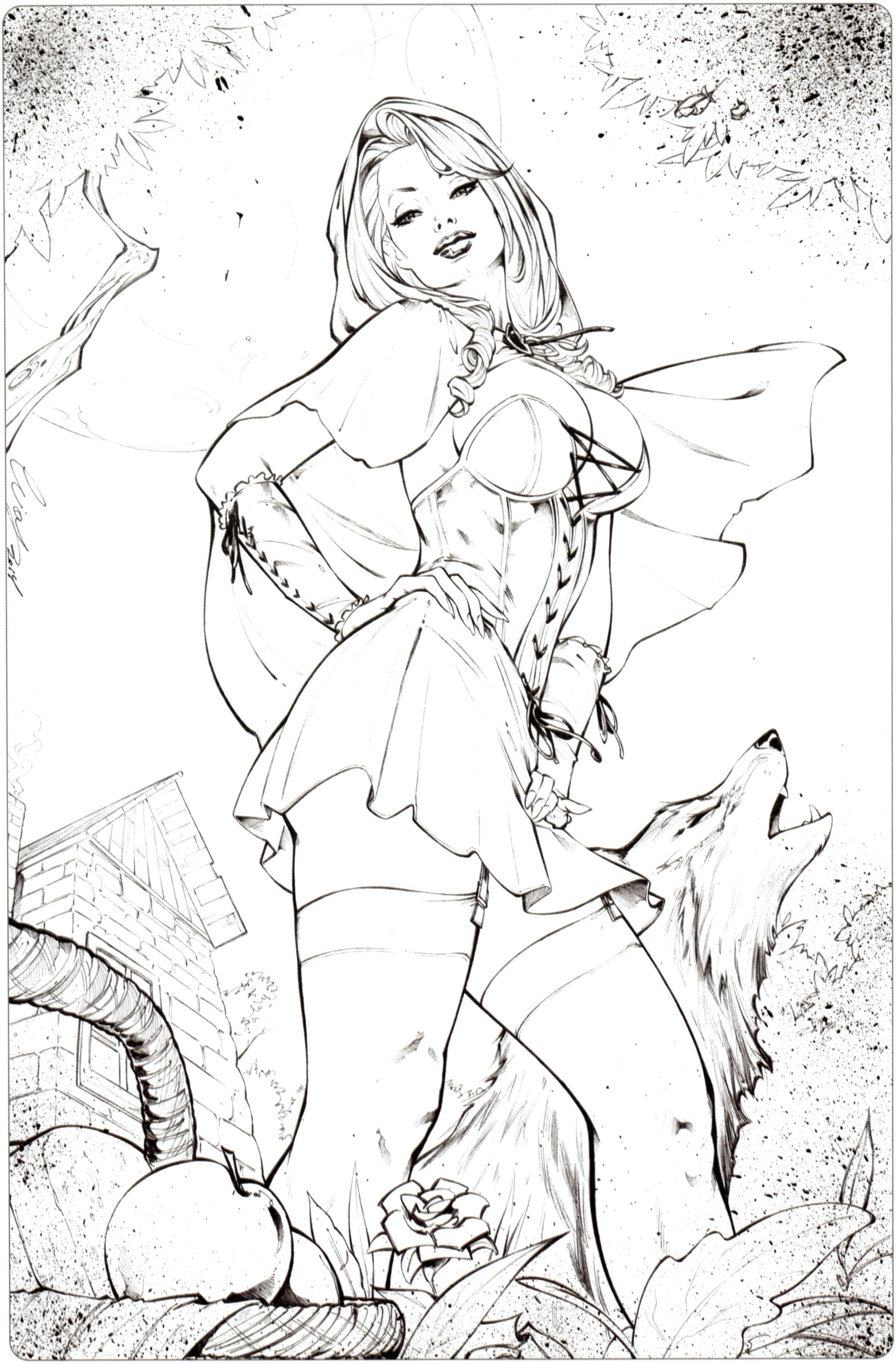

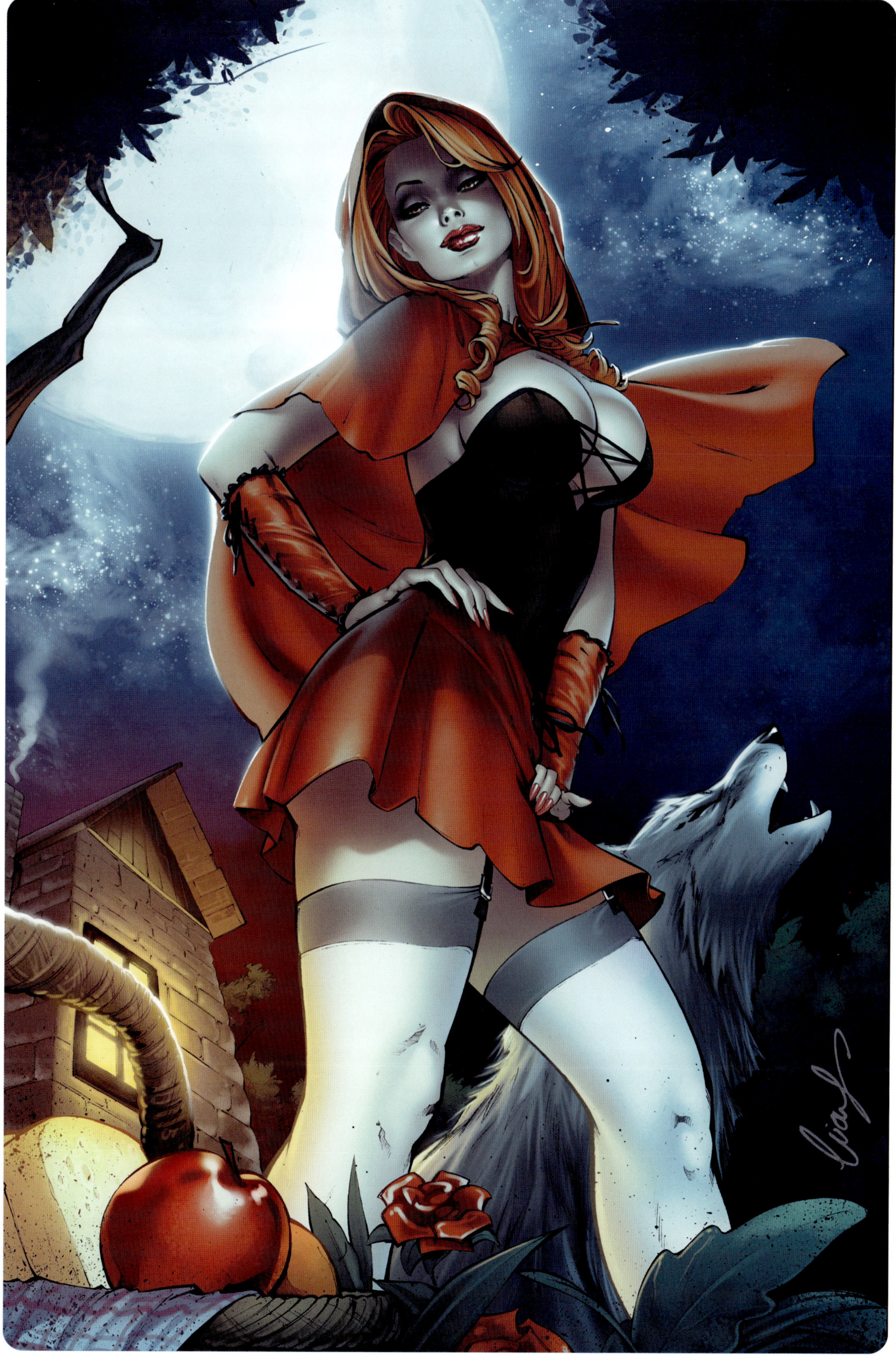

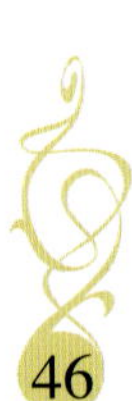

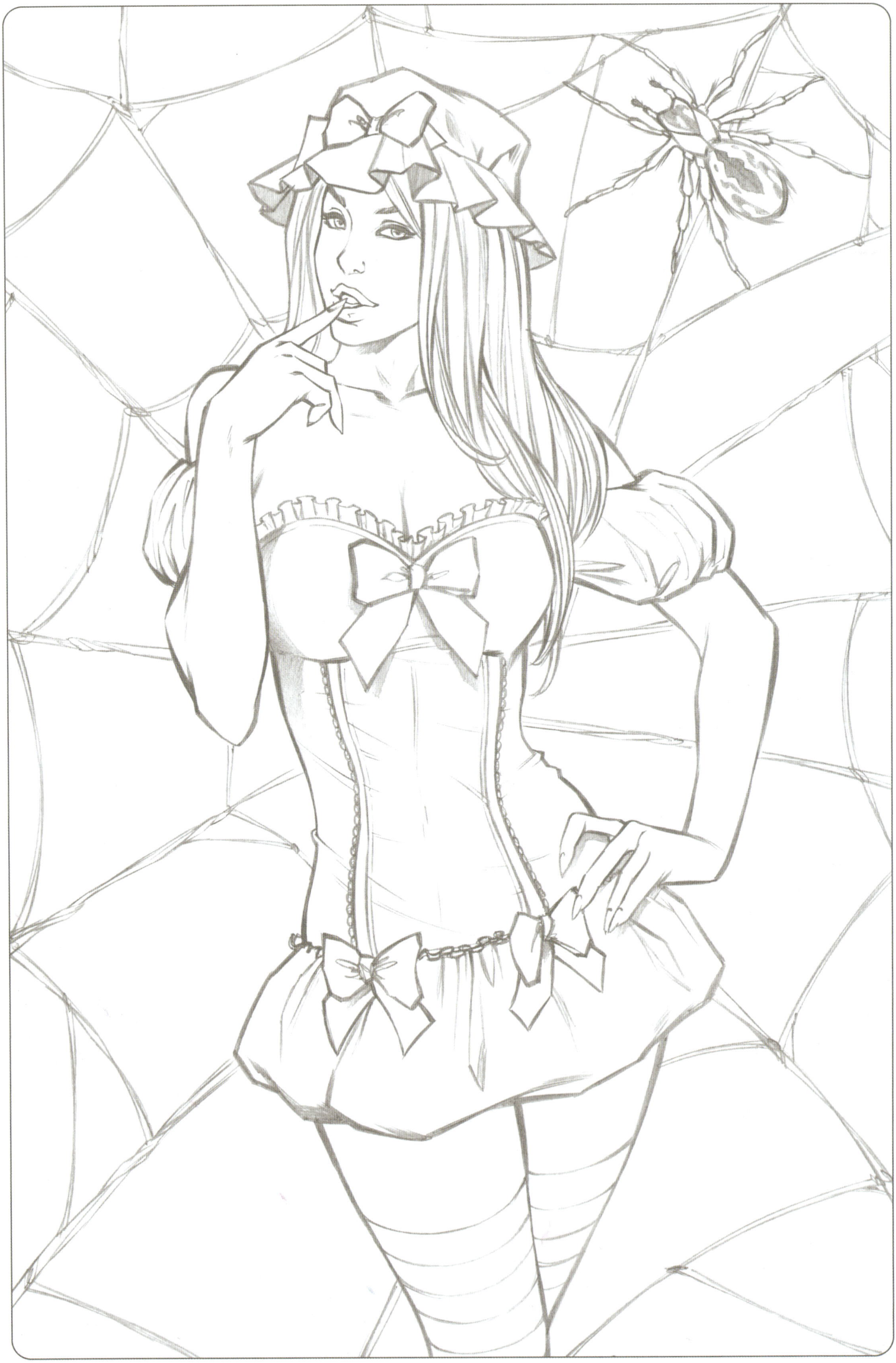

Not so little Miss Muffet

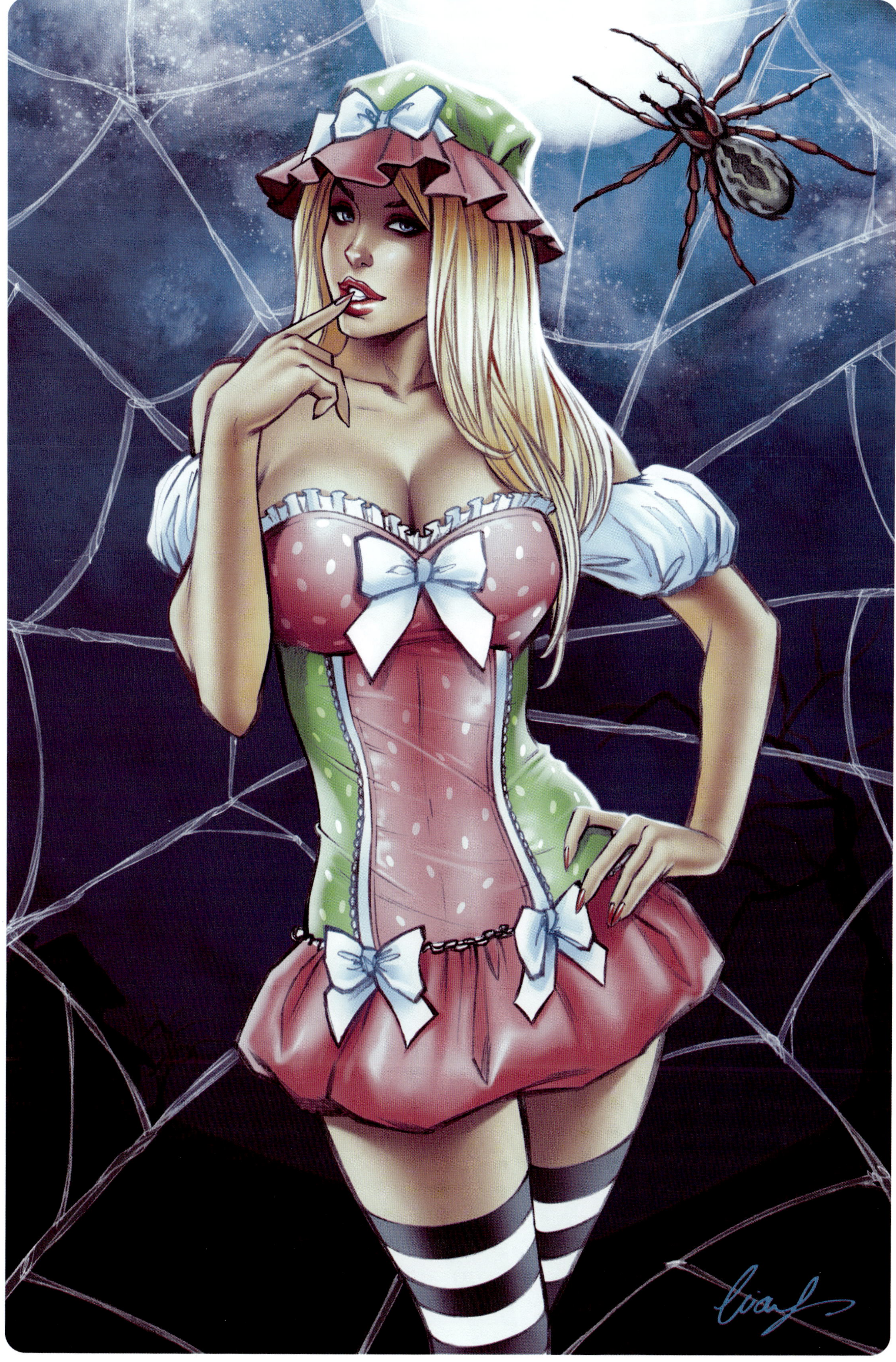

Official website:
www.elias-design.gr
Facebook:
Design of Elias Chatzoudis
Instagram:
eliaschatzoudis
twitter:
Chatgr

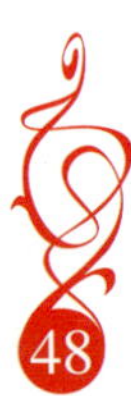

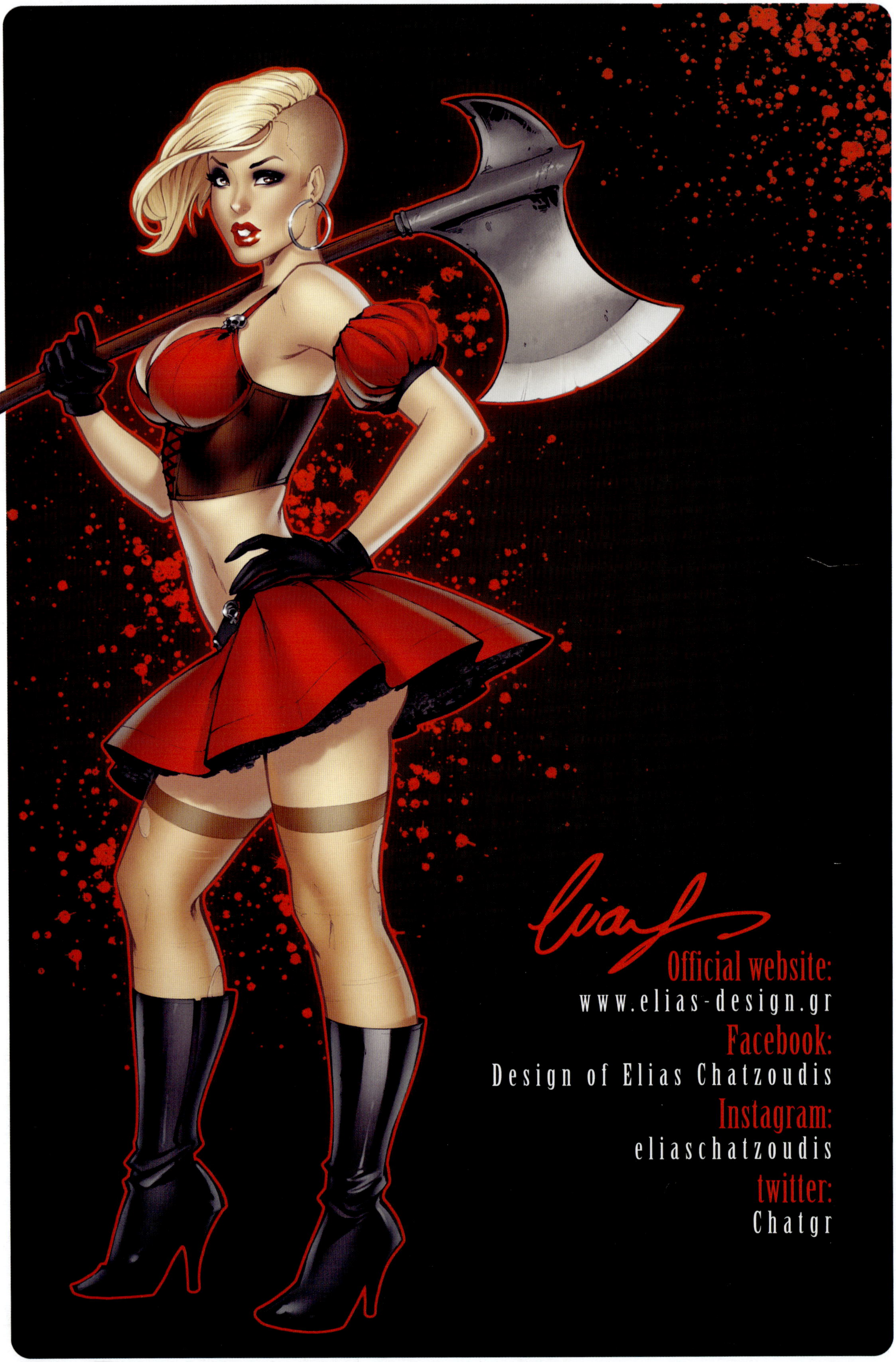